nursery school

outdoor play

picture book

quarter

rattle

scissors

toothbrush

umbrella

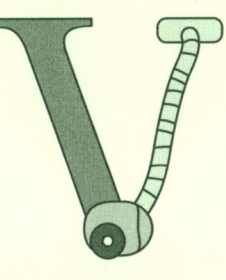
vacuum cleaner

wheelchair

xylophone

yogurt

zipper

保育の
Childcare English
英会話

English for day care workers,
nursery school and kindergarten teachers

Naoko Akamatsu　Yoko Hisatomi
赤松直子◉久富陽子

Houbunshorin
萌文書林

はじめに

　本書は、大学、短大、専門学校で保育を学ぶ人のための英語のテキストとして作成されたものです。

　21世紀は国際化の時代と言われていますが、日本にも現在約150万人を越える外国人の方が生活しており、その数は年々増加しています。在日外国人の中では韓国、中国、フィリピンなどのアジア系の人たちが最も多く、続いてブラジルなどの南米の人たちが続きます。このように多様な文化背景を持った子どもが、現在、日本の保育園や幼稚園に入園することが当たり前になりました。外国人の子どもが入園した場合には、言葉や文化の違いがあるために、保育者は様々な困難を抱え込むことになります。同じように外国人の子どもや保護者も慣れない生活の中で、不安や精神的苦痛を感じる場合が少なくありません。

　このような現実がありながらも、保育者養成の中では、外国人の子どもの保育に関することを学ぶ機会がほとんどないのが現状です。外国人の子どもに関する正しい知識や情報をまったく持たずに保育者になり、外国人の子どもを担任したときには、大きな戸惑いを感じるだけでなく、場合によっては何気ない言葉や態度で外国人の子どもや保護者を傷付けてしまったりすることもあるのです。また、言葉が通じ合えないということから、外国人と関わることに必要以上の緊張感を持ってしまい、あえて関わりを持たないように避けてしまうなどということも起こり得ます。

　保育者を志す学生は、2年あるいは4年間の教育を受けて、保育現場に就職します。その限られた年数の中で、また、現在のカリキュラムの中で、外国人の子どもや保護者とのコミュニケーション、つまりは、異文化間コミュニケーションの基礎を学ぶことができないだろうかと思案しました。そして、学生の専門領域である保育と第一外国語として学ぶ英語という2つの領域を統合することにより、それを実現しようとしたのがこのテキストです。

　テキストの中では、今までの調査研究の中で得られた現場の保育者からのニーズに応えるためにも、また、これから現場に出て行く学生のためにも、外国人の子どもや保護者と関わるときに特に必要性が高いと思われる内容を取り入れました。そして、それを実際のコミュニケーションに生かせるために、英会話での学習を主体にしました。さらに、英会話は、繰り返し耳で聞き、実際に話すことで力がつくことを考え、音声教材を収録したストリーミングサイトを作成しました。

　もちろん、現実の保育現場には、韓国・朝鮮語、中国語、フィリピノ語、スペイン語、

ポルトガル語など様々な言語を母語に持つ子どもたちや保護者がいますので、英語だけを学んでいればよいということではありません。しかし、英語という日本人にとって最も馴染み深い外国語でのコミュニケーションを学んだという実績は、それ以外の言語に触れたときにも必ず自信や意欲につながると思われます。

英語を学ぶということに関して言えば、苦手意識を持っている人もいるかもしれませんが、これから学ぶ英会話が自分の将来の職業と結びつくことが予想できれば、学習目的が明確になり、学習意欲も高まることと思われます。さらにいえば、人と人とのコミュニケーションを基軸にして作り上げてきたこのテキストで学ぶ英会話は、保育現場のみならず、日常生活の中での触れ合いや海外旅行やパーティーなど、人と人とが出会う様々な状況や場所において大いに役立つことでしょう。

人と人とが出会い、理解し合えるということは人生を豊かにします。国際化時代に生きる私たちにとって、さまざまな国の人と出会い、相手を理解し、自分たちをも理解してもらえるようなスキル（能力）を身につけるということは、欠くことのできないことであると共に、自分の人生をさらに豊かにするための喜びにつながると思います。本書が保育を学ぶ人たちの、また、保育現場で保育に携わる人たちの英語コミュニケーションの一助になれば幸いです。

このテキスト作成にあたっては、英語を担当する赤松と保育を担当する久富が長期間にわたって討論を重ね、題材と内容の構成を練ってきました。学習者が楽しく学べるように、問題を解きながら重要な単語や語句を覚えられるようにしたり、英語を学びながらも保育園や幼稚園の生活や子どもの発達が理解できるようにするなどの工夫をこらしたつもりです。その過程にすべて同席してくださった萌文書林の服部雅生氏には貴重なご意見をいただくことができました。心よりお礼申し上げます。また、イラストレーターの西田さんには、私たちが想像していた通りのイラストを描いていただけました。さらに、リー・コーバンさんには日常的な英語表現についてご助言をいただきました。ここに記して感謝申し上げます。

2002年7月

赤松直子／久富陽子

本書付属の音声データの再生方法

『保育の英会話』各Unitの音声（MP3形式）を聴いてみましょう。パソコンやスマートフォン、タブレットなどでストリーミングサイトにアクセスすることですぐに聴くことができます。ここでは、パソコンはWindows11、スマートフォンはiPhone（iOS17）を例に解説します。

●●●●● パソコンで音声を再生する ●●●●●

❶ パソコンのブラウザー（ここではEdgeを使用）のアドレスバーに次のストリーミングサイトのURLをキーボードから入力します。

> **https://houbun.com/audio/077**

※萌文書林のホームページからはストリーミングサイトにアクセスできません。上記URLを直接入力してください。

❷ ストリーミングサイトのページが表示されるので、再生したいTrackの▶をクリックします。アイコンが⏸に変わり、音声が再生されます。

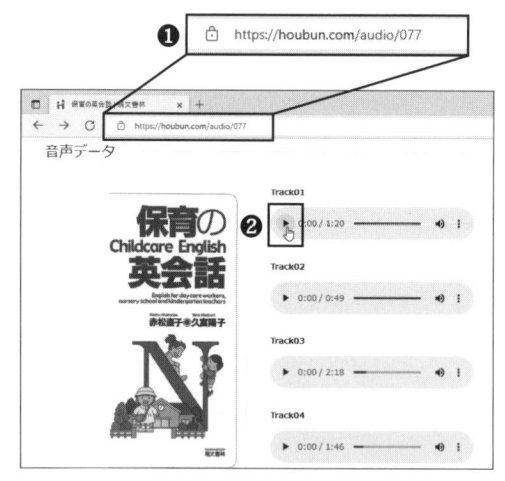

●●●●● スマートフォンやタブレットで音声を再生する ●●●●●

❶ スマートフォンやタブレットの場合、専用のQRコードからストリーミングサイトにアクセスできます。ここでは、iPhoneを例に、QRコードで音声を再生してみます。iPhoneでカメラアプリを起動し、右のQRコードにカメラを近づけます。

❷ 画面上部に「WebサイトQRコード "houbun.com" をSafariで開く」という通知が表示されるので、これをタップします。

◎ストリーミングサイトの
QRコード

  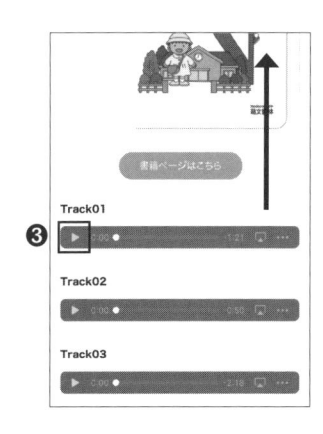

❸ ストリーミングサイトのページが表示されるので、画面を上にスクロールし、再生したい Track の▶をクリックします。アイコンが⏸に変わり、音声が再生されます。

● Android スマホの場合

　Android 9以降のスマホやタブレットの場合は、標準のカメラアプリでQRコードに近づけると、ストリーミングサイトのURLが表示されるので、それをタップすればアクセスできます。また、レンズアプリでも同様にQRコードからアクセスすることができます。

| Column | ストリーミングサイトを ブックマークに保存する |

　音声ファイルを再生するたびにいちいちQRコードを読み取るのは面倒です。ストリーミングサイトをブックマークに保存しておきましょう。ブックマークを使えば、聴きたいときにすぐにアクセスできます。

　iPhoneの場合は、Safariの画面下にある □↑ をタップし、「ブックマークを追加」をタップします。保存先を指定して「保存」をタップします。画面例では「お気に入り」に保存しました。

　Androidの場合は、Chromeの画面右上の ⋮ をタップして画面一番上の☆をタップします。表示が★に変わり、「モバイルのブックマーク」に保存されます。

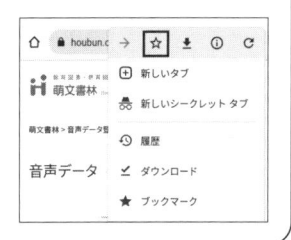

Table of Contents

本書で使われている記号・表記について

 ストリーミングサイトに収録されている会話文・文章・単語を示しています。

 該当の会話文に、入れ替えて練習する単語・語句・表現を示しています。

 会話文の表現や関連表現をとりあげ、表現方法の復習やさらなる表現力をつける
ための練習として示しています。

FIRST STEP TO CHILDCARE ENGLISH Unit 1

簡単な質問と答え　保育園で働く人々　園舎　リスニング

保育の英会話を学ぶ、ファーストステップとして簡単な質問と答えを練習しましょう。また、保育園で働く人々の職業名や保育園の様々な場所を示す語句も学習しましょう。

1. WHAT'S YOUR NAME ?

最初は、簡単な疑問詞を使った質問から始めましょう。これらの質問を使って、学習者がお互いのことを知ることができます。ここでは、テキストの主人公、みなと保育園の保育士片山真理さんに英語の先生が質問しています。みなさんも、間違いなど気にしないで、どんどん英語を使って楽しくコミュニケーションしてみましょう。

Teacher：	What's your name?
Mari：	My name is Mari Katayama .
Teacher：	How do you spell your name?
Mari：	M-a-r-i K-a-t-a-y-a-m-a .
Teacher：	How old are you?
Mari：	I'm 23 years old.
Teacher：	What do you do?
Mari：	I'm a nursery school teacher at Minato Nursery School.
Teacher：	Where do you live?
Mari：	I live in Tokyo .
Teacher：	Where are you from?
Mari：	I'm from Hokkaido .
Teacher：	What's your favorite color?
Mari：	My favorite color is pink .

英語ミニ知識　**How old are you?**　実際はあまり聞かない質問

　日本人は、自分と他者との上下関係を年齢に基づいて考える文化を持っています。その感覚から、たとえ初対面であっても容易に外国人に年齢を尋ねてしまうことがあります。一方、アメリカ人はプライバシーをとても大切にする国民です。年齢もそのプライバシーのひとつです。保育者が子どもたちに年齢を尋ねる場合は特に問題はありませんが、相手が大人の場合、特別な理由もなく年齢を尋ねることは失礼だと考えられます。病院、警察、公的機関などで手続きに必要な場合等は例外です。

　このUnit 1では、みなと保育園で働く人たちを紹介するために、実際的ではありませんが、年齢を尋ねる質問を挿入しています。役割練習のとき、実年齢の表現以外に、"I'm in my 20's." 「私は20代です。」 "I'm in my early 20's / mid 20's / late 20's ." 「私は20代前半 / 20代半ば / 20代後半です。」などの表現もあわせて覚えましょう。

みなと保育園で働いている人たちを紹介しましょう。
前ページの会話文に下記の語句を入れ替えて練習してみましょう。

Akiko Tani 58
nursery school principal
Saitama / Niigata
yellow

Kiyoko Harada 40
head teacher
Chiba / Shizuoka
red

Yoshio Suzuki 28
nursery school teacher
Kanagawa / Tottori
blue

Yayoi Koike 20
part-time assistant
Yokohama-shi / Aomori
purple

Keiko Hayashi 34
school secretary
Urayasu-shi, Chiba / Osaka
orange

Yumi Iida 39
nutritionist
Meguro-ku, Tokyo / Kochi
white

Megumi Takeuchi 43
cook
Mitaka-cho / Fukuoka
black

Ichiro Yamada 56
custodian
Kawasaki-machi / Hiroshima
green

Daisuke Hattori 50
bus driver
Minato-shi / Okinawa
brown

---

nursery school teacher 保育士　　（kindergarten teacher 幼稚園教諭）　　nursery school 保育園　　principal 園長　　head teacher
主任　　part-time assistant パートの（保育）助手　　school secretary 学校事務員　　nutritionist 栄養士　　cook 調理師
custodian 用務員

UNIT 1

9

2. YES‑NO QUESTIONS : DO YOU?   ARE YOU?   CAN YOU?

簡単な質問でも話題が広がります。今度はYes‑No questionsを先生が尋ねています。
英語を話すときはYes／Noをはっきり答えるようにしましょう。

①**Do you ?**　　一般動詞のlike, haveなどを使って質問をしています。真理先生の日常生活の様
　　子、習慣的なこと、嗜好について尋ねることができます。

Teacher ：　　Do you like popular music ? [1]
Mari ：　　　Yes, I do.
Teacher ：　　Do you have a pet ? [2]
Mari ：　　　No, I don't.
Teacher ：　　Do you use the Internet ? [3]
Mari ：　　　Yes, I do.

 上の会話文に語句を入れ替えてパートナーに質問してみましょう。

1）Italian food / snack time / natto / tests / long vacations / children
2）a driver's license / a good memory / a part-time job / a good sense of humor
3）drink coffee / tell jokes / read the newspaper / offer your seat to the elderly

Practice Do you で始まる質問を自由に作ってパートナーに聞いてみましょう。

A：Do you ＿＿＿＿＿＿＿＿＿？　　　　B：Yes, I do. / No, I don't.

driver's license 運転免許証　　memory 記憶力　　have a part-time job アルバイトをする　　sense of humor ユーモアのセンス
offer your seat to the elderly お年寄りに席を譲る　　easygoing 気楽な、暢気な　　Are you a good cook? = Do you cook well?
outgoing 社交的　　talkative おしゃべりな　　right-handed 右ききの　　stubborn 頑固な　　an only child 一人っ子　　punctual
時間厳守の　　a hard worker 熱心に勉強する（働く）人　　creative 創造力のある　　independent 独立心のある　　do magic
tricks 手品をする

② **Are you ?**　　Be動詞のare＋形容詞を使って質問しています。真理先生の国籍、性格、性質などを尋ねることができます。

Teacher：　Are you Japanese ? [1)]
Mari：　　Yes, I am.
Teacher：　Are you easygoing ? [2)]
Mari：　　Yes, I am.
Teacher：　Are you a good cook ? [3)]
Mari：　　No, I'm not.

上の会話文に語句を入れ替えてパートナーに質問してみましょう。

1）Chinese / Korean / Thai / Filipino / Brazilian / Peruvian

2）tall / outgoing / young / talkative / right-handed / stubborn

3）an only child / a punctual person / a hard worker / a big baseball fan / a creative student / an independent girl（or boy）

Practice Are you で始まる質問を自由に作ってパートナーに聞いてみましょう。

A：Are you ＿＿＿＿＿＿＿＿＿？　　　　B：Yes, I am. / No, I'm not.

③ **Can you ?**　　助動詞can＋動詞の原形を使って質問しています。真理先生がどんなことができるか尋ねることができます。

Teacher：　Can you swim ? [1)]
Mari：　　Yes, I can.
Teacher：　Can you play golf ? [2)]
Mari：　　No, I can't.

上の会話文に語句を入れ替えてパートナーに質問してみましょう。

1）ride a bicycle / ski / bake cookies / knit a sweater / do magic tricks

2）soccer / the guitar / table tennis / the piano / the triangle / chess

Practice Can you で始まる質問を自由に作ってパートナーに聞いてみましょう。

A：Can you ＿＿＿＿＿＿＿＿＿？　　　　B：Yes, I can. / No, I can't.

3. SELF – INTRODUCTION

リスニングの練習をしましょう。これは真理先生の自己紹介文です。前ページまでに学習した単語や熟語が使われています。ストリーミングサイトの音声をよく聞いて、空欄に単語を入れましょう。（アルファベットの最初の一文字がヒントになります。）

Hi, everyone! My name is Mari Katayama. I'm a n_____ school teacher. I teach five-year-old children. My class is Kirin-gumi.

_T_____ is my third year at Minato Nursery School. I majored in Early Childhood Education at college. I came here first as a student teacher when I was a freshman and had t_____ weeks of practice teaching.

I'm outgoing and pretty e_____. I'm a punctual person. I'm J_____. I like popular m_____. I often u_____ the Internet. I can swim, s_____ and play the p_____. I can sing k_____ very well.

Working directly with y_____ children all day is a tough job. Some children s_____ to naturally enjoy being with me, but some don't. I feel uncomfortable around those children and wish I c_____ understand them better. I realize that I still need to increase my knowledge of children.

I need to r_____ about children, observe them, talk with them, play with them, and h_____ them. In the process, I will understand better how children grow physically, mentally, emotionally and socially. The more I understand children, the more I will enjoy being with them.

_D_____ you like children? I love them. _C_____ you talk to and enjoy children of all ages? _A_____ you interested in a child-related career? What g_____ have you set for yourself? If you have any q_____ about the children you care for, I can discuss them with you. Now it's your turn. Please introduce yourself!

Practice あなたも自己紹介をしてみましょう。

---

major in 〜を専攻する   Early Childhood Education 幼児教育   student teacher 実習生   practice teaching 教育実習
directly 直接に、じかに   tough 大変な   uncomfortable 気まずい、居心地が悪い   realize 実感する   increase 増やす
knowledge 知識   observe 観察する   process 過程   physically, mentally, emotionally and socially 身体的、心理的、情緒的、
社会的に   related 関連した   career 職業、経歴   care for 世話をする   discuss 論議する   turn 順番、番

4. NURSERY SCHOOL

園舎に関する単語を覚えましょう。みなと保育園の園舎の図を見て、空欄に番号を入れましょう。

__nursery   __gate   __rest room   __kitchen

__room for 1-year-olds   __balcony   __multipurpose hall

__room for 2-year-olds   __storage room   __school office

__room for 3-year-olds   __bathing room   __staff lounge

__room for 4-year-olds   __playground   __entrance

__room for 5-year-olds   __shower room   __terrace

① 沐浴室	② 調理室	③ シャワー室	④ トイレ	⑮ 玄関	⑥ 事務室	⑦ 物置	⑧ 休憩室

⑨ 乳児室（ひよこぐみ）	⑩ 1歳児室（りすぐみ）	⑪ 2歳児室（うさぎぐみ）	⑫ 3歳児室（こじかぐみ）	⑬ 4歳児室（くまぐみ）	⑭ 5歳児室（きりんぐみ）	⑤ ホール

⑱ バルコニー   ⑲ テラス

⑯ 通用門

⑰ 園　庭

Practice 上記の単語を使って次のような練習もできます。at, in, on を使い分けましょう。

A：Where are you ?   B：I'm in the <u>nursery</u>.（図1-14）/ I'm at the <u>entrance</u>.（図15-16）

                                      I'm on the <u>playground</u>.（図17-19）

-year-old …歳の（人）の意を表す　　1-year-old(s) 1歳児（たち）

WELCOME TO MINATO NURSERY SCHOOL! Unit 2

外国人の子どもの入園　あいさつ　デイヴィーの家族紹介　保育室

外国人の子どもが保育園に入園します。初対面の人と出会ったときのあいさつを学びましょう。また、家庭調査票からデイヴィーの家族を理解したり、保育室の中にある様々な物に関する語句も学びましょう。

1. IT'S NICE TO MEET YOU.

園長先生とジェーン・スミスさんが初めて出会い、あいさつを交わします。

Mrs. Tani： Hello. My name is Akiko Tani, the principal here.

Jane： Hello. I'm Jane Smith , David's mother . It's nice to meet you, Mrs. Tani.

Mrs. Tani： It's nice to meet you, too, Mrs. Smith . Where are you from?

Jane： I'm from the United States .

Mrs. Tani： We're very happy to have your son David here .

Jane： Thank you. We're happy to be here, too.

上の会話文に、保護者、子どもの名前、国名を入れ替えて練習しましょう。

1. Pamela Fernandez / Ronaldo's mother / Mrs. Fernandez / the Philippines / son
2. Guo Wen Wang / Mei Hua's grandfather / Mr. Wang / China / granddaughter
3. Bussaba Wannapong / Somchai's mother / Mrs. Wannapong / Thailand / son
4. Jose Perez / Teresa's father / Mr. Perez / Peru / daughter
5. Ana da Silva / Carlos' grandmother / Mrs. Silva / Brazil / grandson
6. Sang Chul Kim / Young Soon's father / Mr. Kim / Korea / daughter

あいさつの練習をしましょう。英語では相手の名前を添えるのが自然です。擦れ違いざまに相手の名前だけを言ってあいさつを交わすこともあります。日本語の「どうも」という感覚です。相手の名前を覚えること、覚えていることを示すことも英語圏のマナーのひとつです。

Greetings	Responses to greetings
Hello, Mrs. Tani.	Hello, David.
Glad to meet you, Jane.	Glad to meet you, too, Ms. Katayama.
Good morning, boys and girls.	Good morning, Mari-sensei.
Good afternoon, children.	Good afternoon, Yoshio-sensei.
Good evening, class.	Good evening, Kiyoko-sensei.

---

grandfather / grandmother 祖父・祖母　　grandson / granddaughter 孫息子・孫娘

2. PLEASE CALL HIM DAVY.

真理先生がジェーンとデイヴィーに出会います。

Mari： Hi, Jane. I'm Mari Katayama, David's class teacher.

Jane： Hi, Ms. Katayama. This is my son David. He's five.

Mari： What should I call him?

Jane： Please call him Davy.

Mari： Davy, call me Mari-sensei.

Davy： OK, Mari-sensei.

Mari： Wow! Very good!

This Is my son David!!

下記の名前と愛称diminutiveを入れ替えて練習しましょう。男の子ならmy son+名前，女の子ならmy daughter+名前と使い分けながら、自由に愛称を選びましょう。

＜Boys' names＞

David → Dave, Davy

Edward → Ed, Eddie, Ted, Teddy

James → Jamie, Jim, Jimmie

Robert → Rob, Robbie, Bob, Bobby

William → Bill, Billy, Will, Willy

＜Girls' names＞

Ann, Anne → Annie, Nan, Nancy

Catherine → Cathy, Kate, Katie, Kitty

Elizabeth → Eliza, Beth, Betty, Liz

Margaret → Maggie, Megan, Peggy

Mary → Mamie, Marie, Polly

英語ミニ知識 英語圏の名前の由来 ─

　Davidの名前の意味は「友、愛すべき人」Janeは「品位がある」です。Edward「幸運な監理人」James「つき従う者」Robert「輝かしい名声」William「決意」Ann「優雅、恩恵」Catherine「清純」Elizabeth「神は幸福そのもの」Margaret「真珠」Mary「神の贈り物」。英語圏の名前にはその語源がはっきりしているものも少なくありません。実際の呼び名には愛称がよく使われます。子どもの頃の愛称にはDavidがDavy, JamesがJamieになるように「小ささ」「親愛感」を意味する指小辞の —y, —ie で終わるものがよく見られます。Bobbyと呼ばれていた男の子が成長とともにBob, EddieがEdというように呼び名が変化しこの指小辞が消えていくことがあります。DavyもいつしかDavidと呼ばれる日がくるかもしれません。

　日本語の〜さんにあたる敬称は男性ならMr. 女性はMrs.（既婚の女性）Miss（未婚の女性）Ms.（既婚・未婚の女性）があります。いずれも姓に冠して用いられます。Jane Smith さんの場合Mrs. Smith, Mrs. Jane smith, また夫Michaelが同席の場合や文書のなかでMrs. Michael Smith と表現できます。Mrs. Jane あるいはMiss Jane と名前だけに敬称をつける言い方は一般的ではありません。Miss Jane あるいは Mr. David の表現は、使用人がジェーンお嬢様、デヴィッドお坊ちゃまと呼ぶニュアンスになります。

3. FAMILY QUESTIONNAIRE　　保育園、幼稚園では家庭調査票を提出してもらいます。
これはデイヴィーの家庭調査票です。よく読んで次ページの質問に答えましょう。

写真 (Recent photograph)	児童氏名 (Child's name) David Smith		性別 (Sex) 男／女 (Male／Female)
	生年月日 (Date of birth) November 10, 20XX　(20XX年11月10日)		
	住所 (Address) #205 Sakura Apartment, 3-1 Sakuramachi, Minato-shi 257-0011 (〒257-0011港市桜町 3-1 さくらアパート205号)		

電話番号 (Home telephone) 049－376－23XX	保護者氏名 (Guardian's name) Michael Smith
血液型 (Blood type) A・B・O・AB	緊急連絡先 (Emergency contact) 049-376-23XX

家族氏名 (Names of family members)	続　柄 (Relation- ship)	年齢 (Age)	職業 (Occupation)	勤務先 (Employer)	職場の電話番号 (Office telephone)
Michael Smith	father (父)	36	computer engineer (コンピューター技師)	TT Computer Service Corporation (TT コンピューターサービス会社)	03－3310－22XX
Jane Smith	mother (母)	32	teacher (教師)	ABC English School (ABC 英会話スクール)	03-5347-98XX

出産した国 (Country of birth) America	妊娠週数 (Duration of pregnancy) 40 weeks (40週)
出生時の体重 (Birth weight) 4050 g	出産の方法 Type of childbirth ☑普通分娩 Normal position □逆子 Breech position □帝王切開 Cesarean section

食べさせていない食品 (Foods not given to child)
□宗教上の理由 (For religious reasons)　☑アレルギー (Allergy)

　　　shrimp (海老)

健康上特に注意すること (Physical limitations and health concerns)
　　He is allergic to shrimp. Please do not feed him shrimp.　(海老によるアレルギーがあります。
給食には海老の除去をお願いします。)

好きな遊び (Your child's interests, hobbies and favorite games)
　　Soccer, baseball and Lego blocks　(サッカー・野球・レゴブロック)

家では何と呼ばれていますか?
(What do you call your child at home ?)　　　Davy (デイヴィー)

主に送迎する人 (Who is responsible for your child's transportation to and from school ?)	mother (母)	送迎の方法 (Type of transportation) ☑徒歩 Walking　□自転車 Bicycle　□車 Car 所要時間 (Transit time)　　10 minutes (10分)

4. QUESTIONS ABOUT DAVY AND HIS FAMILY

デイヴィーと彼の家族についての質問です。答えを書き入れましょう。

1. What's Davy's family name?　　*His family name is Smith.* _____

2. What are Davy's interests or favorite games?　_____

3. Is there any food that Davy can't eat?　_____

4. If yes, what is it?　_____

5. Why can't he eat it?　_____

6. What's Davy's blood type?　_____

7. Who usually drops Davy off and picks him up?　_____

8. How does Davy come to nursery school? _____

9. How long does it take Davy to come to school? _____

10. What's his father's first name?　_____

11. What does he do?　_____

12. Where does he work?　_____

13. What's his mother's first name?　_____

14. What does she do?　_____

15. Where does she work?　_____

16. Which country are the Smiths from, the UK or the USA?

_____

┌─ 保育ミニ知識　外国人児童の増加 ─────────────────────────────

　21世紀は国際化の時代といわれますが、その名の通り日本で暮らす外国人は、増加を続けています。在日外国人は大きく分けると、まず、戦前から日本で暮らしているオールドカマーと呼ばれる人たちと、1990年代以降来日したニューカマーと呼ばれる人たちとがいます。ニューカマーと呼ばれる人たちの多くは、就労のために来日している人たちです。彼らは、初めは単身で来日する場合もありますが、そのうちに家族を呼び寄せたり、日本で結婚、出産し、家庭を持つなど家族単位で日本で暮らすケースが増えています。また、国際結婚も増加していますので、今後はさらに多くの異なった文化背景を持つ子どもたちが幼稚園や保育園に入園することになります。

　そのような子どもたちは、私たち日本人ではわからないような言葉や習慣の違いなど、様々な困難に遭遇していることでしょう。そうした子どもたちが、自分らしさを思う存分に発揮しながら楽しい園生活を送るためには、保育者は子どもたちの文化的な違いを認めながら、必要な援助をしていくことが大切です。

5. INTERVIEW YOUR PARTNER.

あなた自身のことに関する質問です。答えを書き入れましょう。
また同じ質問をパートナーにして、練習しましょう。

1. What's your first name?   *My first name is Yoko.* _____

2. What's your last name?   *My last name is Komatsu.* _____

3. Do you have a nick name?   *Yes, I do.* _____

4. If yes, what is it?   *It is Yoko-chan.* _____

5. What are your interests or favorite games?   _____

6. Is there any food that you can't eat?   _____

7. If yes, what is it?   _____

8. Why can't you eat it?   _____

9. What's your blood type?   _____

10. How do you come to school?   _____

11. How long does it take you to come to school?   _____

12. What's your phone number?   _____

13. What's your zip code?   _____

14. Who is your English teacher?   _____

15. When is your birthday?   _____

16. Do you know on what day of the week you were born?

_____

英語ミニ知識　マザーグースから：曜日唄

Monday's child is fair of face,	月曜生まれの子供は　器量がよい
Tuesday's child is full of grace,	火曜生まれの子供は　品がよい
Wednesday's child is full of woe,	水曜生まれの子供は　悩みがいっぱい
Thursday's child has far to go,	木曜生まれの子供は　遠くに行かなくちゃならない
Friday's child is loving and giving,	金曜生まれの子供は　愛情深くて気前がよい
Saturday's child works hard for living,	土曜生まれの子供は　生活のためにあくせく働く
And the child that is born on the Sabbath day	そして安息日に生まれた子供は
Is bonny and blithe, and good and gay.	健康で快活　親切でほがらかだ

（「マザーグースの唄が聞こえる」藤野紀男著　洋販出版　p.62)

6. MARI–SENSEI'S 5–YEAR–OLDS' CLASSROOM

真理先生の担当する５歳児の保育室です。保育室にある物の単語を覚えましょう。

絵を見て、空欄に番号を入れましょう。

__toy box　　__chair　　__blackboard　　__calendar　　__bookcase　　__cubby　　__wastebasket

__picture　　__coloring book　　__picture book　　__table　　__shoe case　　__door　　__floor

__towel　　__clock　　__window　　__play kitchen　　__wall　　__sink

Practice 上記の単語を使って次のような練習もできます。

A：That's a nice <u>toy box</u>.（図1-20）　　　B：Oh, thank you. I like it, too.

時間　　数　　入園時の所持品

時間や数を表す表現を学びましょう。また、保育園に入園するときに保護者に用意してもらう所持品に関する語句を学びましょう。

 1. PLEASE COME TO SCHOOL AT 8:00.

真理先生がジェーンさんに登園の時間を伝えます。

Mari ： Please come to school at 8:00 tomorrow morning.

Jane ： OK. We'll come at 8 o'clock .

 時計を見ながら、時間を言ってみましょう。時間を入れ替えて練習しましょう。

8 : 00	8 : 05	8 : 10	8 : 15
eight	eight oh-five	eight ten	eight fifteen
eight o'clock	five after eight	ten after eight	a quarter after eight

8 : 20	8 : 25	8 : 30	8 : 35
eight twenty	eight twenty-five	eight thirty	eight thirty-five
twenty after eight	twenty-five after eight	half past eight	twenty-five to nine

8 : 40	8 : 45	8 : 50	8 : 55
eight forty	eight forty-five	eight fifty	eight fifty-five
twenty to nine	a quarter to nine	ten to nine	five to nine

Practice 時間の尋ね方・答え方

A ： What time is it?　　　B ： It's eight thirty. / It's half past eight.

2. WHAT TIME?

次の質問に答えて時間を書き入れましょう。また、パートナーにも質問し時間を書き取り、
答えを確認しましょう。

	〈you〉	〈your partner〉
What time do you get up ?	I get up at _____ 6：30 .	7：10
1. do you have breakfast?	I have breakfast at ___：___	___：___
2. do you leave the house?	I leave the house at ___：___	___：___
3. do you get to school?	I get to school at ___：___	___：___
4. do you have lunch?	I have lunch at ___：___	___：___
5. do you have a snack?	I have a snack at ___：___	___：___
6. do you go home?	I go home at ___：___	___：___
7. do you have supper?	I have supper at ___：___	___：___
8. do you take a bath?	I take a bath at ___：___	___：___
9. do you go to bed?	I go to bed at ___：___	___：___
10. do you get up on Sundays?	I get up at ___：___	___：___
11. did you go to bed last night?	I went to bed at ___：___	___：___

Practice What timeで始まる質問を自由に作って、パートナーに聞いてみましょう。

A：What time _____? 　　　　B：_____.

適当な語句を選んで空欄に書き入れましょう。

noon　midnight　A.M.　P.M.

1. Cinderella went home at _____
2. I always get up at 7：00 _____
3. I usually have supper at 7：00 _____
4. Our lunchtime starts at _____

保育ミニ知識　時間に厳しい日本の保育者!?

　外国人の保護者にインタビューをしたところ (注)、外国人の保護者は日本の保育者に対して「優しい」「真面目」など非常に高い評価をしていました。ただし、"日本の保育者は時間にとても厳しい"という声がありました。時間に対する考え方にも、文化の違いがあります。たとえば、約束の時間を守ることよりも神様にお祈りを捧げる時間を大切に考える、時間に遅れることが日常的であるという文化や習慣を持つ民族がいます。そのような時間に対する考え方を持つ保護者には、時間を守る必要性が感じられないことがあるのかもしれません。また、慣れない異国で生活することはとても大変なことなので、時間に遅れがちになる保護者もいるのでしょう。保育者からすれば、保育のためにも子どものためにも時間を守ってもらうことは必要なことなのだと思いますが、外国人の保護者が日本の保育者を信頼し、安心して子どもをあずけてくれていることのほうが、何倍も大切なことなのだということも思い出してほしいと思います。

(注)「外国人の子どもの保育－親たちの要望と保育者の対応の実態」萌文書林 1997年

3. FOR TOMORROW, COULD YOU BRING A PAIR OF INDOOR SHOES?

真理先生はジェーンさんに登園時間と保育園に持ってきてもらいたい物を伝えます。

Jane： What time should we come tomorrow?

Mari： Please arrive at school by 8:30 .

Jane： OK. By 8:30 .

Mari： This is a list of things Davy will need at nursery school. A school bag, a change of clothes, pajamas...

Jane： Oh, so many things! I can't get them all at once.

Mari： Don't worry, Jane. Take your time and get them little by little.

Jane： Thank you.

Mari： For tomorrow, could you bring a pair of indoor shoes ?
The rest can wait, but he'll need the indoor shoes right away.

Jane： Sure.

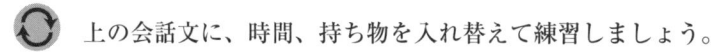 上の会話文に、時間、持ち物を入れ替えて練習しましょう。

8:10 ／ a pair of pajamas

8:15 ／ three pairs of underpants and three undershirts

8:30 ／ a pair of chopsticks

8:40 ／ a thermos

8:45 ／ a cup and a toothbrush

8:50 ／ two futon sheets

英語ミニ知識　「ふとん」について

　futon は外来語としてアメリカに存在しますが、アメリカでは日本のような綿入りの布団は一般的に使用されませんので、布団や布団カバーを説明するときは実物を見せながら話すことが必要です。アメリカではベッドが使用され、その場合、まずマットレス mattress を敷き、その上にシーツ fitted sheet、次に上掛けシーツ flat sheet、次に毛布 blanket、その上にベッドカバー bedspread を広げて使用します。キルトあるいはコンフォーター quilt / comforter と呼ばれるキルティングの上掛けもあります。掛け布団を英訳するのは同じものがアメリカにないので難しいのですが、掛け布団は blanket が毛布以外にも広い意味での上掛けを意味しますので blanket を使います。敷布団は sleeping mat と表現すればニュアンスが伝わります。布団カバーは、外来語の futon を用い、futon sheet や fitted futon sheet という表現が考えられます。なるべく実物を見せたり購入できる場所を示すなど、外国人の保護者に具体的に説明することが大切です。

---

a pair of 一組の、一足の　　indoor shoes 上履き　　a change of clothes 着替え　　at once 同時に、すぐに　　take your time ゆっくり時間をかける　　right away すぐに　　chopsticks 箸　　thermos 水筒(魔法瓶)　　toothbrush ハブラシ
at 8 o'clock 8時に　　by 8 o'clock 8時までに

4. NUMBERS

ストリーミングサイトの音声を聞き、数の発音を練習しましょう。

1	2	3	4	5	6	7	8	9	10
one	two	three	four	five	six	seven	eight	nine	ten

11	12	13	14	15	16	17	18	19	20
eleven	twelve	thirteen	fourteen	fifteen	sixteen	seventeen	eighteen	nineteen	twenty

21	22	30	40	50	60	70	80	90	100
twenty-one	twenty-two	thirty	forty	fifty	sixty	seventy	eighty	ninety	one hundred

101	200	300	1,000	10,000
one hundred one	two hundred	three hundred	one thousand	ten thousand

100,000	1,000,000	10,000,000	100,000,000	1,000,000,000
one hundred thousand	one million	ten million	one hundred million	one billion

次の数字を読んでみましょう。また、ノートに書き表してみましょう。

24	78	125	740	908
3,044	6,495	56,117	98,000	25,476
234,990	376,740	1,980,300	2,000,010	9,876,543

Practice 足し算、引き算、掛け算、割り算の数式を読んでみましょう。

Addition	$5 + 3 = 8$	Five plus three equals eight.
	$7 + 4 = 11$	Seven plus four is eleven.
Subtraction	$9 - 2 = 7$	Nine minus two equals seven.
	$6 - 6 = 0$	Six minus six is zero.
Multiplication	$8 \times 6 = 48$	Eight times six equals forty-eight.
	$4 \times 7 = 28$	Four times seven is twenty-eight.
Division	$9 \div 3 = 3$	Nine divided by three equals three.
	$20 \div 10 = 2$	Twenty divided by ten is two.

5. MINATO NURSERY SCHOOL REQUIRED SUPPLIES

保育園に入園するときに保護者に用意してもらうものです。それらを示す単語を覚えましょう。絵を見て、空欄に番号を入れましょう。また次ページの「保育園からのお知らせ」も読んでみましょう。

__school bag   __smock   __undershirt   __shorts   __jacket   __handkerchief   __chopsticks
__toothbrush   __futon sheet   __cup   __indoor shoes   __swim trunks   __swim cap
__small plastic bag   __sleeping mat   __hand towel   __raincoat   __cap   __hat   __shoe bag

保育園からのお知らせ (Notice from Minato Nursery School)
Dear Parents,
The school will provide a parent-teacher communication notebook. Parents should label all personal belongings with the child's name. Pajamas, towels, and futon sheets must be brought home on weekends for washing, as there is no laundry service available at the school.
Akiko Tani
Principal

__face towel   __cleaning cloth   __rain boots   __thermos   __backpack   __blanket

__tissues   __shoes   __chopstick box   __clothes bag   __underpants   __pants   __vest

__pajamas   __swimsuit   __bath towel   __apron   __socks   __box lunch   __umbrella

DIRECTIONS

Unit 4

保育園の周辺マップ　道順・案内

ジェーンさんが場所や道順を尋ねています。様々な場所の名称や方向を示す語句を覚え、前置詞を使って場所や道順を説明する表現を学びましょう。

1. PLACES AROUND MINATO NURSERY SCHOOL

ストリーミングサイトの音声を聞きながら、みなと保育園の周辺マップの中にある場所を指差しましょう。

また、場所を表す単語を覚えましょう。

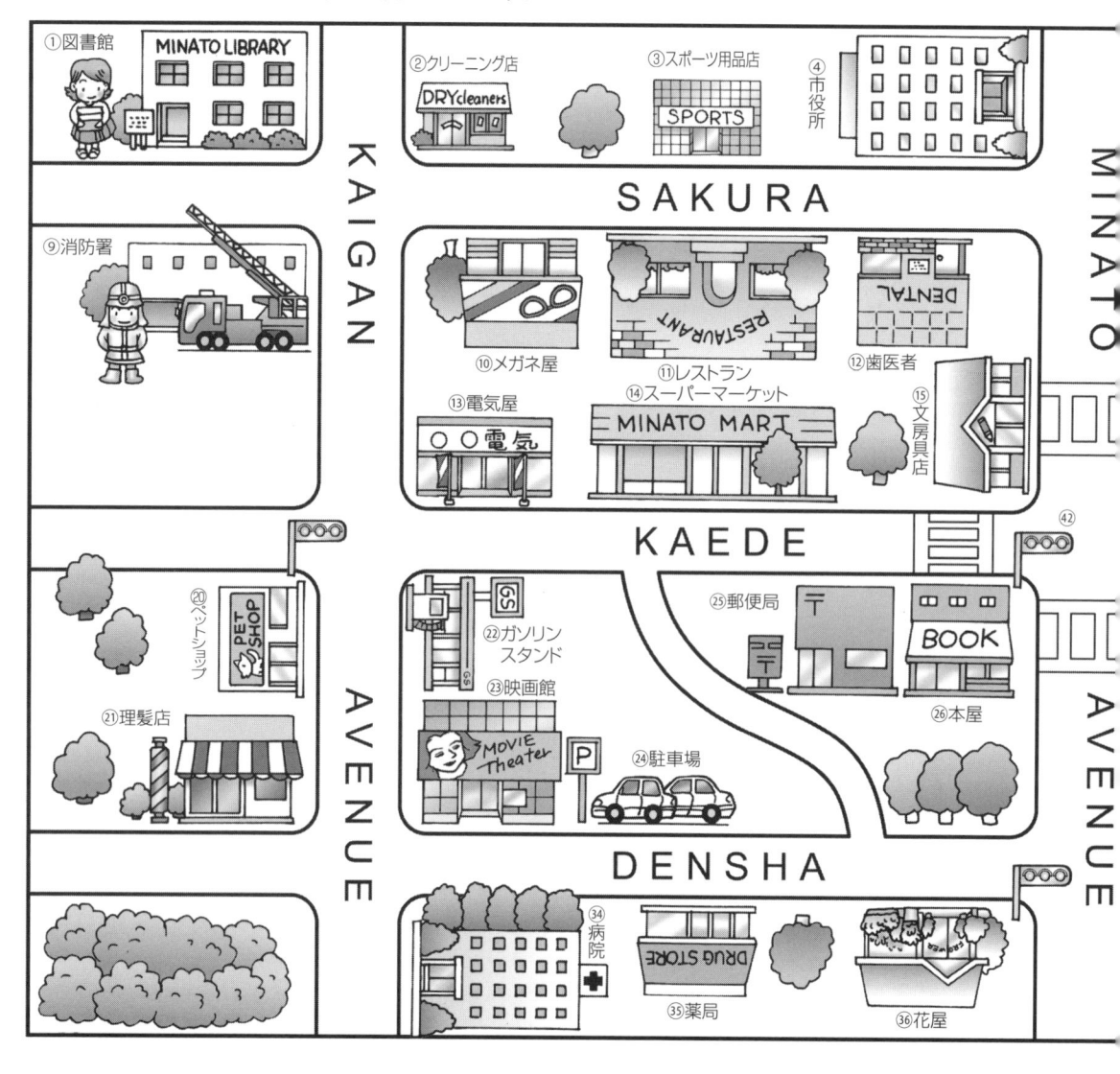

---

traffic light 信号　　crosswalk 横断歩道　　street / avenue 通り

① library ② dry cleaners ③ sporting goods shop ④ city hall ⑤ toy store ⑥ shrine
⑦ after-school childcare center ⑧ apartment building ⑨ fire station ⑩ eyeglass store ⑪ restaurant
⑫ dentist ⑬ electronics store ⑭ supermarket ⑮ stationery store ⑯ Minato Nursery School
⑰ park ⑱ convenience store ⑲ beauty salon ⑳ pet shop ㉑ barber shop ㉒ gas station
㉓ movie theater ㉔ parking lot ㉕ post office ㉖ bookstore ㉗ health center ㉘ elementary
school ㉙ bakery ㉚ shoe store ㉛ coffee shop ㉜ bank ㉝ community center
㉞ hospital ㉟ drugstore ㊱ flower shop ㊲ video shop ㊳ police station ㊳ train station
㊵ nursing home ㊶ bus stop ㊷ traffic light ㊷ crosswalk

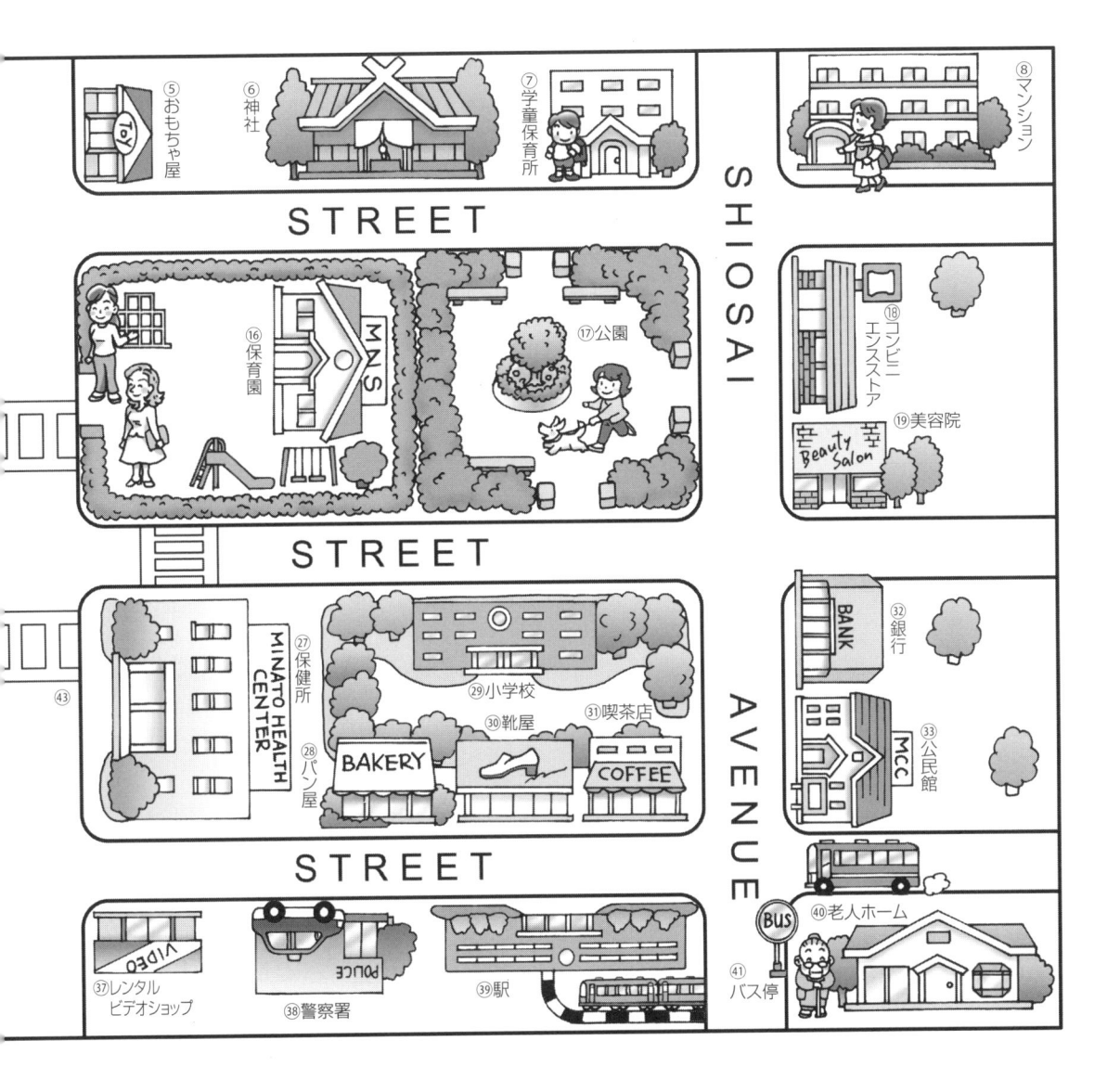

2. WHERE IS THE POST OFFICE?

前置詞を使って場所を示す表現を学びます。

A：Where is the post office?

B：It's **next to** the bookstore.

A：Where is the restaurant?

B：It's **between** the dentist **and** the eyeglass store.

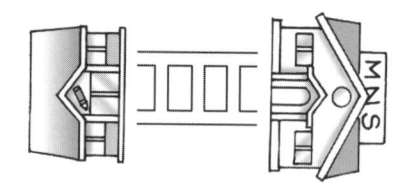

A：Where is the stationery store?

B：It's **across from** Minato Nursery School.

A：Where is the hospital?

B：It's **around the corner from** the drugstore.

前ページの地図を見ながら、下記の場所を示す前置詞を使い、質問に答えましょう。

1. Where is city hall?

across from

2. Where is the shrine?

between

3. Where is the community center?

next to

4. Where is the bakery?

around the corner from

3. IS THERE A SHOE STORE NEARBY?

ジェーンさんはデイヴィーの上履きを買おうと靴屋さんの場所を真理先生に尋ねます。

Jane： Mari-sensei, I'd like to buy indoor shoes .

Is there a shoe store nearby?

Mari： Yes, there is.

Jane： Where is the shoe store ?

Mari： It's across from the train station .

 上の会話文にジェーンさんの用件と行き先を入れ替えて練習しましょう。

1. buy some Japanese stamps ／ a post office ／ next to the bookstore

2. get some crayons ／ a stationery store ／ across from Minato Nursery School

3. have lunch ／ a restaurant ／ between the dentist and the eyeglass store

4. watch a movie ／ a movie theater ／ next to the gas station

5. get some medicine ／ a drugstore ／ between the hospital and the flower shop

6. exchange some US dollars for Japanese yen ／ a bank ／ across from
the elementary school

7. have my VCR repaired ／ an electronics store ／ next to the supermarket

地図を見て、空欄に行き先、適当な前置詞を入れ、さらに語句を入れ替えて練習しましょう。

1. have my hair cut ／ a_____ ／ _____ the bank.

2. rent some videos ／ a_____ ／ _____ the police station.

3. buy some groceries ／ a_____ ／ _____ the stationery store
_____ the electronics store.

---

medicine 薬　　exchange 両替する　　have my VCR repaired ビデオデッキを修理してもらう(have+目的語＋過去分詞　主語の
意志で〜してもらう、させるの使役、受態の意味を表す)　　groceries 食料品、雑貨

4. TURN LEFT AT THE SECOND TRAFFIC LIGHT.

ジェーンさんは真理先生に靴屋さんまでの道順を尋ねます。

Jane： Could you tell me the way to the shoe store ?

Mari： OK. Go straight down along Minato Avenue.
Turn left at the second traffic light .
It's on the left , next to the bakery .

Jane： Thank you for the directions. We'll go there right away.

上の会話文に、行き先、行き方などの語句を入れ替えて練習しましょう。

1. drugstore ／ down ／ right ／ second traffic light ／ the left ／ between the flower shop and the hospital
2. library ／ up ／ left ／ first corner ／ the right ／ across from the fire station
3. park ／ down ／ left ／ first traffic light ／ the left ／ behind the nursery school

地図を見ながら、様々な場所への道順を説明しましょう。また、出発点を変えて道順を説明しましょう

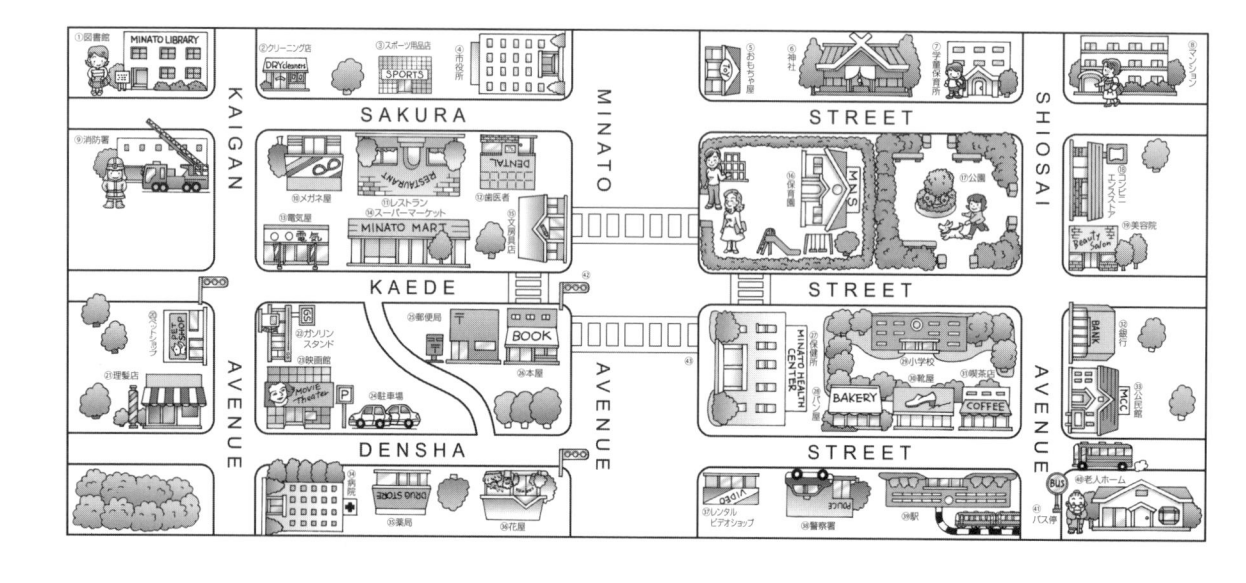

Practice 最寄りの駅からあなたの学校までの道順を英語で説明してみましょう。

5. JANE'S LETTER TO HER PARENTS

文章を完成する問題です。ジェーンさんがアメリカの両親へ、日本での生活を綴った手紙を書きました。空欄に下記の単語を選んで入れましょう。

| worried workplace everything viewing grandchild helpful different ~~perfect~~ start packed |

April 30

Dear Mom and Dad,

How are you? I hope you're fine. We're doing well and gradually getting used to this new life. It's a _____perfect_____ time to arrive in Japan. The weather is getting warmer. April is a new _____ 2 for new students, new careers and newcomers like us. Michael's co-workers took us to the park for "Cherry-blossom _____ 3 ," known as hanami, several weeks ago. Japanese people were enjoying eating, drinking, singing and dancing under the beautiful blossoms. We enjoyed this festive mood.

Michael has found his new _____ 4 busy, but challenging. He signed a contract for two years with TT Computer Service Corporation. As for Japanese food, he enjoys most kinds, but not sashimi. Last night he tried it and thought it tasted funny. He doesn't like commuting here. Every morning he is _____ 5 in a train on the way to work.

Last week, I had some trouble. They didn't collect my garbage. Garbage disposal here is very _____ 6 from America. In Japan, garbage is divided into three categories: burnable, non-burnable, and recyclable. I didn't know this.

I have good news. You are going to have another _____ 7 in December. To tell the truth, I am _____ 8 about my delivery here. I mean the language. I speak very little Japanese. However, I've heard many Japanese obstetricians speak English well enough to discuss my pregnancy. I think _____ 9 will be OK.

Davy started nursery school. He really needs friends to play with. He is an active, playful, curious and creative boy, just like any other child. He enjoyed his first day very much. His teacher, Mari, is studying English and is a very _____ 10 person.

Love,

Jane

---

gradually 次第に　　get used to ～に慣れる　　weather 天候　　co-worker 同僚　　blossoms（開）花　　festive お祭り気分の　contract 契約書　　as for ～に関しては　　commute 通勤する　　garbage disposal ごみ処理　　be divided into ～に分別される　　burnable 可燃性の　　non-burnable 不燃性の　　my delivery 私の出産　　obstetrician 産科医　　pregnancy 妊娠　curious 好奇心旺盛の

DAVY MEETS HIS CLASSMATE TAKASHI **Unit 5**

紹介　　子どもの遊び　　園庭の遊具

デイヴィーをクラスメイトに紹介します。他者を紹介するときの表現を学びましょう。また、子ども
の遊びや園庭の遊具を表す語句を学びます。

1. LET'S PLAY WITH BLOCKS.

真理先生がデイヴィーをクラスメイトに紹介します。
子どもたちはデイヴィーを遊びに誘います。

Mari ：　　Takashi, this is Davy , your new friend.
　　　　　　He comes from America . He' ll be in Kirin-gumi.

Takashi ：　Hi, Davy . Let's play with blocks .

Davy ：　　OK, let's. Sounds good .

上の会話文に子どもの名前、出身国、遊びなどの語句を入れ替えて練習しましょう。

Ronaldo
He / the Philippines
play tag
fun

Mei Hua
She / China
play with clay
neat

Young Soon
She / Korea
play house
nice

Teresa
She / Peru
play dress-up with dolls
okay

Carlos
He / Brazil
play with toy trains
cool

Somchai
He / Thailand
put a jigsaw puzzle together
hard

neat すてきな　　cool カッコいい　　hard むずかしい

2. WHAT DO YOU WANT TO DO?

たかしがデイヴィーを外遊びに誘います。

Takashi ： Davy , let's go outside and play.
Davy ： What do you want to do?
Takashi ： I want to play in the sandbox .
Davy ： OK. Get a shovel and a pail .
Takashi ： Let's make a big castle .

 子どもの名前、遊び、遊具などを入れ替えて練習しましょう。

Ronaldo
play catch
a ball
I've got one

Mei Hua
jump rope
a jump rope
Here

Young Soon
play hide-and-seek
your shoes
I'm coming

Teresa
ride a unicycle
yours
I love this!

Carlos
fly a kite
a kite string
Wait

Somchai
play on the seesaw
your cap
Why?

---

sandbox 砂場　　pail バケツ　　castle お城　　kite string 凧糸

3. PLAYGROUND

園庭の遊具等を表す単語を覚えましょう。園庭の絵を見て空欄に番号を書き入れましょう。

__swing　　__slide　　__sandbox　　__monkey bars　　__chin-up bar　　__jungle gym　　__climbing pole

__unicycle　　__bicycle　　__tricycle　　__wading pool　　__bench　　__shovel　　__pail　　__ball

__jump rope　　__seesaw　　__kite　　__fence　　__tree　　__nest　　__water fountain　　__flower bed

__vegetable planter　　__tulip　　__rabbit hutch　　__toy storage shed

Practice 上記の単語を使って次のような練習もできます。on と in を使い分けましょう。

A：Let's play on the <u>swing.</u>（図1-7）　　A：Let's play in the <u>sandbox</u>.（図8-9）

B：OK, let's.　　　　　　　　　　　　　　B：OK, let's.

4. CHILDREN ON THE PLAYGROUND

子どもの遊んでいる動作を表す表現を学びましょう。絵を見て単語の適当な番号を書き入れましょう。

① jump rope   ② throw a ball   ③ catch a ball   ④ kick a ball   ⑤ bounce a ball   ⑥ slide down the slide   ⑦ swing on the swing   ⑧ climb a tree   ⑨ climb up/down a climbing pole   ⑩ ride a tricycle   ⑪ catch a butterfly   ⑫ dig a hole   ⑬ make sand pies   ⑭ play in the water   ⑮ hang on the monkey bars   ⑯ play Superman

1. (　　　)　　2. (　　　)　　3. (　　　)　　4. (　　　)

5. (　　　)　　6. (　　　)　　7. (　　　)　　8. (　　　)

9. (　　　)　　10. (　　　)　　11. (　　　)　　12. (　　　)

13. (　　　)　　14. (　　　)　　15. (　　　)　　16. (　　　)

DROPPING DAVY OFF AND PICKING HIM UP Unit 6

登園・降園　　天候　　感情を表す表現　　時制

真理先生とジェーンさんの登園・降園時の会話です。天候・感情・状態を表す表現を学びましょう。

1. IT'S SUNNY TODAY.

登園時、ジェーンさんと真理先生が話をしています。

Mari ： Good morning, Jane and Davy.
　　　　It's sunny today.
Jane ： Good morning, Mari-sensei.
　　　　Yes, it's a sunny day.
Mari ： How are you today, Davy?
Davy ： Fine. How are you?
Mari ： I'm fine .

Jane ： I have to go. Good-bye, Davy.
Davy ： Bye, Mommy.
Jane ： Have a good day !

Good morning!!

上の会話文に天候などの語句を入れ替えて練習しましょう。

1. cloudy ／ great ／ Have a nice day
2. rainy ／ good ／ Have fun
3. windy ／ pretty good ／ Have a lot of fun
4. snowy ／ well ／ Enjoy
5. hot ／ OK ／ Enjoy yourself
6. warm ／ all right ／ Have a good time
7. cool ／ so-so ／ Be a good boy
8. cold ／ not so bad ／ Listen to your teacher today

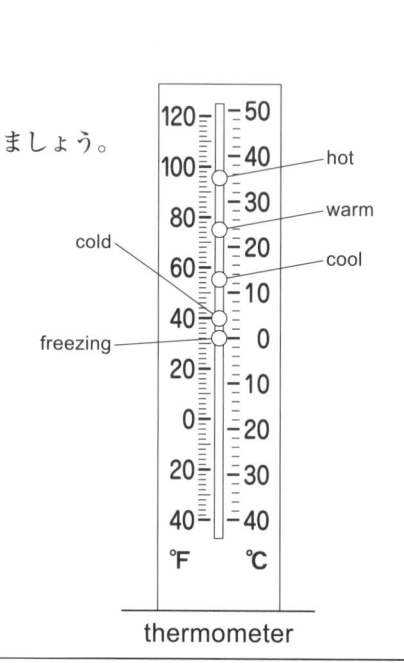

thermometer

hot
warm
cold
cool
freezing

mommy（幼児語)ママ、おかあちゃん（イギリス英語ではmummy)

2. HE COULD BE NERVOUS BECAUSE HE IS NEW.

降園時、真理先生がジェーンさんにデイヴィーの園での様子を伝えます。

Jane： How was Davy today?

Mari： He was a good boy, but he looked nervous today.

Jane： Did he?

Mari： Yes, but please don't worry too much. He could be nervous because he is new.

Jane： Do you think so?

Mari： Yes. But he will gradually adjust. He just needs a little more time.

Jane： I hope so.

Mari： I'm sure he'll be all right.

 上の会話文に子どもの様子を表す表現を入れ替えて練習しましょう。

1. looked uneasy
   be uneasy

2. seemed shy
   be shy

3. seemed lonely
   be lonely

4. cried and seemed upset
   be upset

5. stayed inside all day
   be staying in

6. kept quiet all day
   be not talking

---

nervous 緊張している，落ち着かない　　could be nervous 緊張することもある、ありえる　　adjust 順応する　　uneasy 不安
がる　　shy 恥ずかしがる　　lonely 寂しい、心細い　　upset 動揺する、困る　　stay inside all day 一日中室内にいる

3. HOW WAS DAVY TODAY?

子どもの感情や状態を表す単語を学びましょう。下記の単語を適当と思われる絵の下に書き入れましょう。

Jane： How was Davy today?

Mari： Oh, he was nervous .

surprised	sleepy	~~excited~~	sick	~~grumpy~~	hungry	angry	
nice	happy	thirsty	sad	cold	scared	tired	full	bored

1. _____

2. _____

3. _____

4. _____

5. _____

6. _____

7. _____

8. _grumpy_

9. _____

10. _____

11. _____

12. _____

13. _excited_

14. _____

15. _____

16. _____

sick 病気の、かげんの悪い　　grumpy 不機嫌な、気難しい　　scared 怖がって、おびえて

4. HOW WAS YOUR DAY TODAY?

ジェーンさんがデイヴィーに保育園でどのような一日を過ごしたのか尋ねます。デイヴィーが現在形で答え、真理先生が過去形に訂正しながら話します。

Jane ： How was your day today?

Davy ： I make an origami balloon .

Mari ： Yes, he made an origami balloon this afternoon.

動詞を過去形に書き直しましょう。例にならい、
上記の会話に入れ替えて練習をしましょう。

〈現在形〉		〈過去形〉
1. sing many songs	⟶	sang many songs
2. get my pants muddy	⟶	got his pants muddy
3. paint a picture	⟶	_____
4. read fairy tales	⟶	_____
5. do fingerplays	⟶	_____
6. play the castanets	⟶	_____
7. blow soap bubbles	⟶	_____
8. catch three big snails	⟶	_____
9. knead the clay	⟶	_____
10. put away the crayons	⟶	_____
11. break a toy	⟶	_____
12. make up with Takashi	⟶	_____
13. eat all my lunch	⟶	_____
14. sleep well	⟶	_____
15. brush my teeth very well	⟶	_____
16. lose a tooth	⟶	_____

Practice 上の会話文に合うような他の例を自分で作ってみましょう。

A：I _____ .   B：Yes, he _____ this afternoon.

Practice 動詞を変化させ、過去形、現在形（3人称単数）、現在進行形を練習しましょう。

A：He sang many songs.   B：He sings many songs.   C：He is singing many songs.

---

get my pants muddy ズボンを泥だらけにする   fairy 妖精   fairy tales おとぎ話   do a fingerplay 手遊びをする   make up with ～と仲直りする   put away 片付ける   lose a tooth 歯が抜ける

5. DAVY USUALLY . . . .

ジェーンさんが真理先生に家族のことを話しています。アンダーラインの動詞が正しいものは
〇で囲み、不適当なものは×を記し、正しい動詞を書き入れましょう。

"Davy usually go→ _____ to bed at eight o'clock. My husband Mike or I
always read→ _____ him bedtime stories. Davy often ask→ _____ Mike
for piggyback rides. Davy sometimes want→ _____ to stay up late. We never
let→ _____ him do so. Mike always say→ _____ ,'8 o'clock, it's time for bed.' "

頻度を表す副詞always ／ usually ／ often ／ sometimes ／ rarely ／ neverから適
当なものを選び、自分自身のことを表現しましょう。

1. I sometimes read the newspaper.
2. I _____ wear jeans.
3. I _____ go to karaoke.
4. I _____ cook supper.
5. I _____ meet famous people.
6. I _____ have breakfast.
7. I _____ grow vegetables.
8. I _____ study English.

6. HAVE YOU EVER SEEN A GHOST?

デイヴィーが真理先生に現在までの経験「〇〇したことがありますか？」と尋ねます。現在完
了形（have you+過去分詞）を使います。

Davy： Have you ever seen a ghost?

Mari： Yes, I have. I've seen many.

Davy： Really? Where have you seen them?

Mari： Davy, have you been to Tokyo Disneyland?

Davy： No, I haven't. Have you seen ghosts there?

Mari： Yes, I have. I've seen them in the haunted mansion.

動詞の原形を正しい過去分詞形に直しましょう。また、語句を入れ替えてパートナーに尋ねて
みましょう。

1. Have you (be) _____ to Okinawa / a class reunion / a concert?

2. Have you (have) _____ snake soup / turkey / a barbecue?

3. Have you (swim) _____ in the ocean / a swimming pool / a puddle?

4. Have you (ride) _____ a horse / a roller-coaster / an ambulance?

5. Have you (play) _____ Scrabble / rugby / computer games?

6. Have you (hear) _____ your English teacher sing / scream / speak French?

---

piggyback ride 肩車、おんぶ　　class reunion 同窓会　　turkey 七面鳥　　ambulance 救急車　　scream 悲鳴をあげる

7. CLOTHING FOR ALL KINDS OF WEATHER

天候に合わせて、下線部に適切な衣服などを表す語句を入れましょう。

wool tights　running shoes　straw hat and sandals　umbrella　shorts

1. Put on your _____.　　It's hot and sunny.

2. Wear _____.　　It's snowing.

3. I'll wear my _____.　　It's too hot for slacks.

4. Where are my _____?　　It's nice and warm. Let's go jogging.

5. Take an _____.　　It's going to rain.

Let's sing "THE CLEAN-UP SONG" and "THE GOOD-BYE SONG"

おかたづけの歌、降園時のさようならの歌を一緒に歌ってみましょう。これは、THE FARMER IN THE DELL「谷間のお百姓さん」という歌の替え歌になっています。

THE FARMER IN THE DELL

Sung to the tune of THE FARMER IN THE DELL

CLEAN-UP SONG

Everyone, clean up

Everyone, clean up

Heigh-ho, way to go

Everyone, clean up

GOOD-BYE SONG

It's time to say good-bye

It's time to say good-bye

Heigh-ho, away we go

It's time to say good-bye

英語ミニ知識　**Tooth Fairy**（歯の妖精）

アメリカの子どもたちに伝わる歯の妖精についての文を読んでみましょう。

When they lose a tooth, many American children put the tooth under their pillows when they go to sleep at night. They believe the Tooth Fairy will come while they sleep, take the tooth, and leave some money for them in its place. Although most children stop believing in the Tooth Fairy before they stop losing teeth, many continue to pretend they believe in order to get more money.

保育者の仕事

みなと保育園の保育者、真理先生（5歳児）、よしお先生（1歳児）、きよ子先生（0歳児）の仕事を見てみましょう。子どもの年齢の違いによる保育者の仕事の違いも比べてみましょう。

1. MARI-SENSEI'S DAILY SCHEDULE

真理先生の保育者としての仕事を、ある一日を例にとって見てみましょう。

In the morning

8:00　Arrival：

Mari-sensei meets the children and checks the parent-teacher communication notebooks.

Outdoor playtime：

She plays tag, dodge ball, and other games, or plays in the sandbox.

Clean-up time：

She puts away the toys and the playground equipment.

10:00　Toilet time：

She has the children use the rest room.

Circle time：

She has the children sit in a circle, has a morning assembly, and takes attendance.

Music and movement time：

She plays the piano, sings, and dances with the children.

Creative time：

She helps the children do crafts, paint, or draw pictures.

Story time：

She reads picture books or tells stories illustrated with picture cards.

In the afternoon

12:00　Lunchtime：

She prepares for lunch, serves tea, and eats with

the children.

1:30　Nap time：

She helps the children put on their pajamas,

makes beds, and tucks them in.

She keeps track of the parent-teacher communication

notebooks, has a meeting with the staff, or updates the

daily record of the class.

3:00　Snack time：

She wakes the children and helps

them get dressed.

She gives the children snacks and drinks.

Free playtime：

She plays inside or outside.

Departure：

She helps the children get ready for going home

and meets the parents who pick them up.

5:00　Clean-up time：

She cleans the classroom.

---

playground equipment 遊具　　have the children use the rest room 子どもたちをトイレに行かせる（have+ 目的語＋原形不定詞～
させる、使役の表現）　　sit in a circle 円になって座る　　stories illustrated with picture cards 紙芝居　　help children put on
pajamas 子どもたちがパジャマを着るのを手伝う　　tuck them in （子どもたち）を寝具でくるむ　　keep track of ここでは、
（連絡帳に）記入するの意　　daily record of the class 保育日誌

2. WHAT DOES MARI-SENSEI DO IN THE 5-YEAR-OLDS' CLASS?

真理先生（5歳児担当）の保育です。日本語に訳して5歳児担当の保育者の仕事を理解しましょう。

1. She does a fingerplay.
2. She teaches the children.
3. She hugs the children.
4. She sings and dances.
5. She helps the children take care of the rabbits.
6. She does a paper-puppet show for the children.
7. She does a storytelling apron show for the children.
8. She displays paintings on a classroom bulletin board.

真理先生と子どもたちのかかわりを考えながら、右の文章の記号を空欄に書き入れましょう。

1. When children cut their knees, _____
2. When children have a fever, _____
3. When children have runny noses, _____
4. When children get dressed, _____
5. When children cry, _____
6. When children have a fight, _____
7. When children whisper to Mari-sensei, _____
8. When children hide themselves behind the drapes, _____

a. she hears both sides.
b. she finds them.
c. she helps them with their buttons.
d. she whispers secrets in their ears, too.
e. she takes their temperature.
f. she dries their tears.
g. she puts Band-Aids on them.
h. she wipes their noses.

(保育ミニ知識) ペープサート、エプロンシアター ————————

　ペープサートとは、画用紙などに動物の絵などを書き、切り取って、棒をつけたものです。また、エプロンシアターとは、保育者が着けたエプロンを舞台にした人形劇です。

3. WHAT DOES YOSHIO-SENSEI DO IN THE TODDLERS' CLASS?

よしお先生（1歳児担当）の保育です。
正しい語句に○をつけ、1歳児担当の保育者の仕事を理解しましょう。

1. He lifts the toddlers up and （down / dawn）.
2. He （helps / eats） the toddlers with their lunch.
3. He （washes / holds） hands with the toddlers when they walk.
4. He （plays / prays） blocks with the toddlers.
5. He （needs / wipes） their sticky hands and dirty feet.
6. He puts the toddlers on the （potties / trash cans）.
7. He takes the toddlers for a walk in the （stroller-cart / cradle）.
8. He （pulls / breaks） the wagon.
9. He （sells / reads） a book to the toddlers.
10. He （types / repeats） what the toddlers say.
11. He （tears / shows） picture cards and picture books to the toddlers.
12. He （changes / borrows） their underwear.
13. He keeps the classroom safe and （comfortable / uncomfortable）.
14. He helps the toddlers （wash / clap） their hands before lunch.
15. He encourages the toddlers to rinse their （mouths / rice）.

英語ミニ知識　子どもを表す英語表現　Toddlers sit on the potties, not babies！
子どもを表す英語表現は、a child / children が一般的ですが、やや砕けた表現でa kid / kids も日常会話ではよく使われます。赤ちゃんを表すことばはa baby / babies が一般的です。また、乳児、幼児を表すことばにはan infant / infants や a toddler / toddlers があります。toddlerはよちよち歩きの幼児（1歳前後から2歳くらいまで）を意味し、infantには7歳未満の小児、幼児を指すこともありますが、通常は歩行前の乳児を意味します。お母さんに抱きかかえられているうちはinfant, 歩き出すと toddler と呼び名が変わります。

sticky ねばねばする　　dirty 汚れている　　stroller-cart 散歩用手押し車　　underwear 肌着類

4. WHAT DOES KIYOKO-SENSEI DO IN THE INFANTS' CLASS?

きよ子先生（0歳児担任）の保育です。
正しい語句に○をつけ、0歳児担当の保育者の仕事を理解しましょう。

1. She feeds the babies（formula / cornflakes）.
2. She（cooks / wipes）their drool.
3. She uses（baby soap / teething rings）when she bathes the babies.
4. She tries（burping / washing）the babies after each feed.
5. She rocks the babies to（sleep / cool）.
6. She plays（peek-a-boo / Peter Pan）.
7. She tickles their（tummies / cribs）.
8. She cleans their bottoms on the（changing table / diaper pail）.
9. She needs baby（food / wipes）when she changes diapers.
10. She sings（lullabies / rock 'n' roll）to the babies.
11. She plays（a music box / cards）for the babies.
12. She holds the babies（insecurely / securely）.
13. She（talks / jumps）to the babies.
14. She plays with a（rattle / jump rope）.
15. She carries the babies in her arms and goes for a（walk / drink）.

Let's sing one of the popular English lullabies.

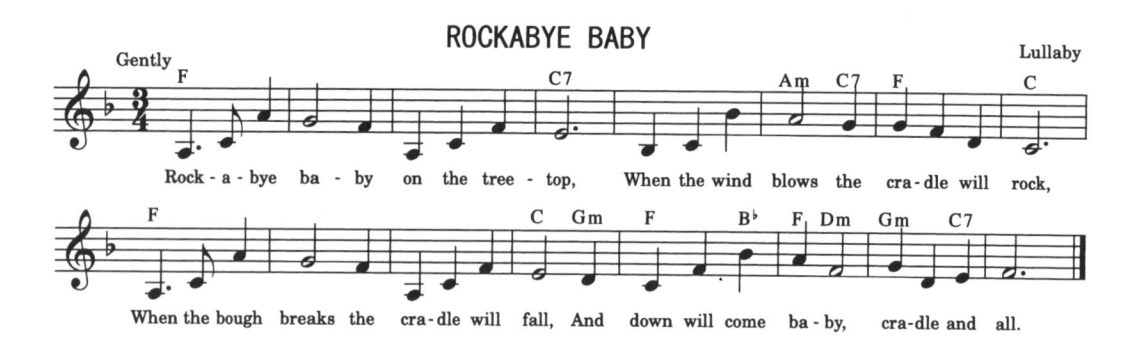

ROCKABYE BABY

cf. p.77　drool よだれ　tummy（幼児語）おなか、ぽんぽん

5. LET'S TRY ORIGAMI CRAFTS

真理先生は風船の折り方をデイヴィーに教えます。図を参考に英文を読みながら折り紙で
風船を折ってみましょう。

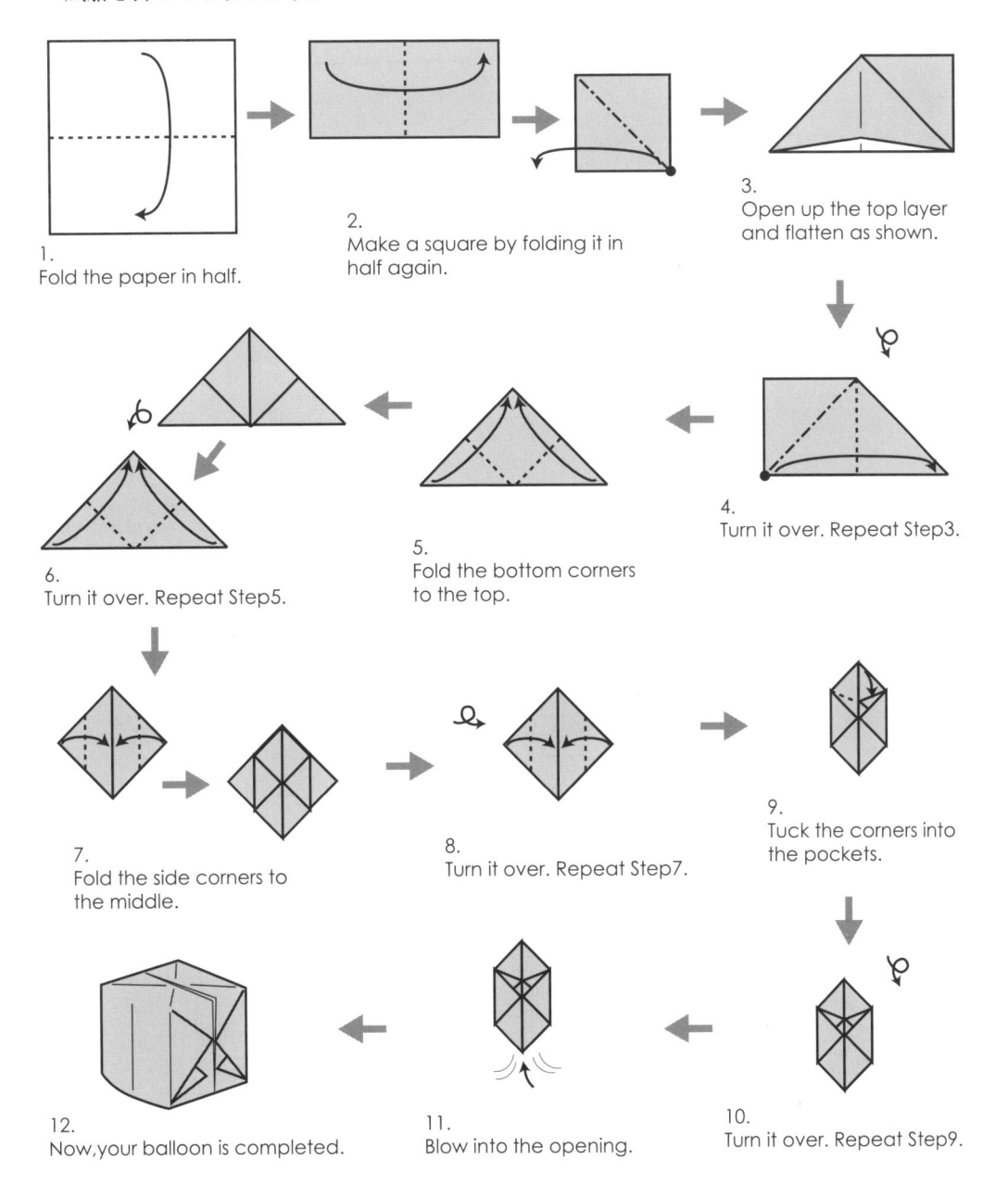

1.
Fold the paper in half.

2.
Make a square by folding it in half again.

3.
Open up the top layer and flatten as shown.

4.
Turn it over. Repeat Step3.

5.
Fold the bottom corners to the top.

6.
Turn it over. Repeat Step5.

7.
Fold the side corners to the middle.

8.
Turn it over. Repeat Step7.

9.
Tuck the corners into the pockets.

10.
Turn it over. Repeat Step9.

11.
Blow into the opening.

12.
Now,your balloon is completed.

fold 折る   square 正方形   flatten 平らにする   turn over 裏返す   bottom corners 底部の両端   the top 中央上部
side corners 左右のかど   the middle 中央   tuck into the pockets ポケットの内側へ折り込む   opening 穴   complete =
(finish)完成する

LUNCHTIME

 **Unit 8**

食事　調理法　分量　嗜好

保育園での昼食風景から、食品や献立、調理法などの英語表現を学びましょう。また、分量や好き嫌いを表す表現を練習しましょう。

 1. WASH YOUR HANDS, PLEASE.

子どもたちが楽しみにしている昼食が始まります。

Mari : It's lunchtime. Everyone, wash your hands, please.

Davy : We all did.

Mari : All right. Let's have lunch. Itadakimasu.

Davy : Itadakimasu.

Mari : Davy, what do you have today?

Davy : Oyakodonburi.

Mari : Your Japanese is good!

Davy : Thank you. This is yummy.

Mari : Be careful with the soup. Don't spill it.

保育ミニ知識 食文化の違い

食事に関する文化の違いも様々です。何を食べるのか、どうやって食べるのか、また、いつ食べるのかといったように、食品、調理法、味付け、食べる時のマナー、禁食（主には宗教的な理由によって禁止されている食品）など、その違いをあげればきりがありません。ここでは、特に園生活にかかわることをあげておきます。まず、一番にあげられるのが禁食です。イスラム教では豚肉を食べることが禁止されていることは有名ですが、細かく刻んだハムや出し汁に使われている場合にも取り除くようにしなければいけません。豚肉を食べることは神様に背くことであるため、誤って食べさせてしまった場合の保育者の責任は大変重いものになります。また、日本ではお茶碗を手に持って食べるようにしつけられますが、逆に韓国などでは、お茶碗やお皿を持ち上げることは無作法であるとみなされます。また、必ずご飯には汁物をかけて食べる、手食の習慣があるなど、文化によって様々な食べ方のマナーがありますので、そのような食べ方をしている子どもたちを安易に「しつけができてない」などと思い込まないようにしたいものです。また、日本のお弁当についての考え方は、外国人の保護者には伝わりにくいもののひとつのようです。遠足のお弁当に生のお寿司を持ってきてしまったり、スナック菓子が入っているだけであったりと、驚いてしまう保育者も多いのですが、お弁当という習慣のない外国人の保護者の立場からみれば無理からぬことです。

---

yummy （幼児語）おいしい

2. I DON'T LIKE GREEN PEPPERS.

真理先生はデイヴィーにお代わりをよそってあげたり、嫌いな食べ物も少しずつ食べられるように言葉をかけていきます。

Davy： Mari-sensei, look! I'm finished.

Mari： You are a good boy. Would you like to have some more meatballs ?

Davy： Yes, please.

Mari： Oh, you haven't touched your salad yet.

Davy： I don't like green peppers . I can't eat it.

Mari： Well, how about trying to eat just half of it today?

Davy： OK.

 飲み物、食べ物、分量などを入れ替えて練習しましょう。

1. tea ／ celery ／ a（one）third
2. fried chicken ／ potatoes ／ two thirds
3. milk ／ cucumbers ／ a（one）fourth
4. corn soup ／ lettuce ／ one bite
5. curry and rice ／ carrots ／ a few bites
6. vegetable stew ／ cabbage ／ a bit

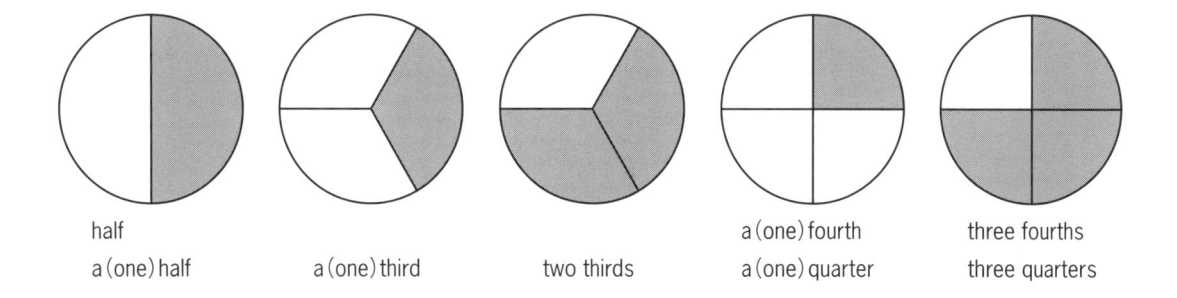

half a（one）half	a（one）third	two thirds	a（one）fourth a（one）quarter	three fourths three quarters

---

Would you like to have some more? ～をもう少しいかが。　　green pepper ピーマン　　How about ～はどうですか。　　one bite 一口

3. WHAT DAVY LIKES AND DOESN'T LIKE

デイヴィーが好きなものと嫌いなものをあげてみました。
子どもの嗜好の傾向と英語での表現を学びましょう。

DAVY LIKES：

peanut butter, banana shakes, hot chocolate, strawberries, Mommy's baking powder biscuits and oven fried chicken, toy trucks, frogs, the zoo, nursery school, his grandpas and grandmas, Daddy and Mommy, and his birthday.

DAVY LIKES TO：

watch animated cartoons, have a snack, play with his friends, be held in Mommy's arms, ride on Daddy's shoulders, play tricks, go to the toy store, cook with Mommy, and go up to high places.

DAVY DOESN'T LIKE：

green peppers, celery, carrots, shrimp, stomachaches, slugs, snakes, bees, ghosts, rainy days, thunder and lightning, darkness, or nasty kids.

DAVY DOESN'T LIKE TO：

keep still, walk through crowds, wear tight clothes, wear too many clothes, be put to bed too early, see Mommy get irritated, or see his parents fight.

Practice あなたが好きなもの、嫌いなものをlike+名詞、like+to不定詞を使って書いてみましょう。

_____

_____

_____

_____

_____

---

animated cartoons アニメの漫画　　slug ナメクジ　　thunder and lightning 雷と稲光　　keep still じっとする

4. LUNCH MENU

給食でよく使われる食品や料理の単語を学びましょう。
みなと保育園のある１週間の給食献立表です。空欄に下記の日本語の番号を書き入れましょう。

	Lunch	Snack
Monday	__beef stew（__beef __ onions __ carrots __ potatoes __peas）__rice__miso soup（__tofu__wakame seaweed）	__pudding or __jello __rice cracker
Tuesday	__sandwiches（__ham__lettuce__cucumbers__eggs __tomatoes__strawberry jam__butter） __corn soup（__corn__milk）	__grilled onigiri
Wednesday	__spaghetti with meat sauce（__pork） __potato salad（__potatoes__carrots）	__pumpkin cake
Thursday	__chicken and egg on rice（__chicken__egg） __miso soup（__daikon radish__fried tofu）	__yogurt __wafer
Friday	__fried salmon（__salmon） __rice__spinach with sesame dressing	__sweet rice cake with soybean flour
Saturday	__cream stew（__bacon__onions__carrots__potatoes __green beans）__rolls	__apple pie

1. 鮭のフライ
2. とうもろこし
3. ロールパン
4. ヨーグルト
5. サンドイッチ
6. インゲン
7. 牛肉
8. ご飯
9. 親子どんぶり
10. おせんべい
11. ハム

12. フルーツゼリー
13. 人参
14. 油揚げ
15. ウエハース
16. ビーフシチュー
17. きゅうり
18. 牛乳
19. アップルパイ
20. 焼きおにぎり
21. クリームシチュー
22. スパゲティーミートソース

23. トマト
24. 苺ジャム
25. じゃが芋
26. ベーコン
27. ポテトサラダ
28. ほうれん草の胡麻和え
29. グリーンピース
30. わかめ
31. 黄粉餅
32. 玉ねぎ
33. 大根

34. プリン
35. 味噌汁
36. 豆腐
37. 卵
38. 鶏肉
39. 豚肉
40. バター
41. 鮭
42. レタス
43. コーンスープ
44. かぼちゃのケーキ

5. HOW DO YOU SAY OYAKODONBURI IN ENGLISH?

献立の英語表現を学びましょう。

真理先生が、給食の献立の英語表現をジェーンさんに尋ねています。

Mari： How do you say oyakodonburi in English?

Jane： Chicken and egg on rice .

日本語にあう英語の表現を選び空欄に書き入れましょう。また、上記の会話にこれらの語句を入れ替えて練習しましょう。

1. 肉じゃが ＿＿＿＿　　　　　　　a. clear soup

2. かき玉汁 ＿＿＿＿　　　　　　　b. rice with chicken and vegetables

3. とんかつ ＿＿＿＿　　　　　　　c. grilled eggplant

4. 高野豆腐煮 ＿＿＿＿　　　　　　d. ginger pork saut é

5. かやくご飯 ＿＿＿＿　　　　　　e. beaten egg soup

6. おでん ＿＿＿＿　　　　　　　　f. braised hijiki seaweed

7. だし巻き卵 ＿＿＿＿　　　　　　g. simmered mackerel in miso

8. しょうが焼き ＿＿＿＿　　　　　h. simmered freeze-dried tofu

9. 焼きナス ＿＿＿＿　　　　　　　i. pork cutlets

10. サバのみそ煮 ＿＿＿＿　　　　　j. oden stew

11. すまし汁 ＿＿＿＿　　　　　　　k. braised meat potatoes

12. ひじきのいため煮 ＿＿＿＿　　　l. rolled omelet

絵を見て、調理方法を書き入れましょう。

cut	peel	steam	boil	fry	pour	microwave	grate

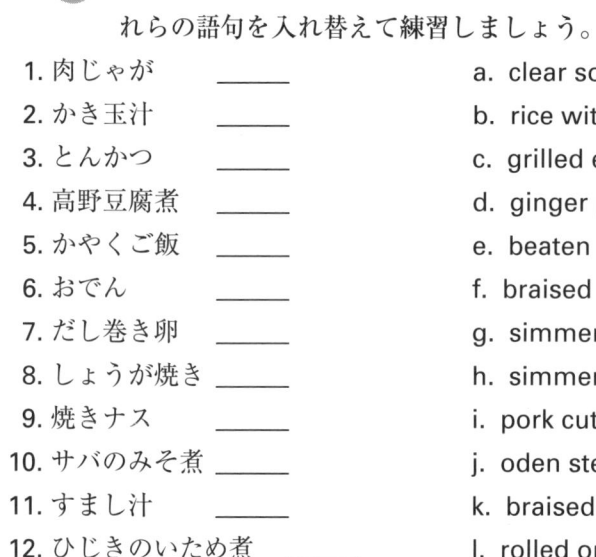

1. ＿＿＿＿　　　2. ＿＿＿＿　　　3. ＿＿＿＿　　　4. ＿＿＿＿

5. ＿＿＿＿　　　6. ＿＿＿＿　　　7. ＿＿＿＿　　　8. ＿＿＿＿

grill 網焼きする　　saut 少量の油で手早くいためる　　braise 油でいため、鍋に蓋をして少量の水でとろとろに煮込む
simmer 沸騰させないようにしながら、ぐつぐつ時間をかけて煮る　　stew 柔らかくなるまで、時間をかけて煮る

6. JANE'S SPECIAL RECIPES — DAVY'S FAVORITE ONES!

英語でレシピを読んでみましょう。ジェーンさんは、デイヴィーの好物、オーブンフ
ライドチキンとベーキングパウダービスケットを作ります。

OVEN FRIED CHICKEN　Serves 6 （6人分）

子どもたちが大好きなポテトチップやコーンフレイクを使い、オーブンで焼くフライドチキン。

What you need：

1.5 kg	cut up chicken （breasts, legs, thighs mixed）
1/2 cup	melted butter
2 cups	crushed potato chips or cornflakes or rice cereal
1 clove	mashed garlic
1/2 teaspoon	salt

In a bowl, mix chicken, salt and garlic.　Dip chicken in butter, then roll in chips.　Place in shallow baking
pan.　Don't let sides touch.　Sprinkle with leftover butter and crumbs.　Bake at 375℉, about 1 hour.

BAKING POWDER BISCUITS　16 biscuits （16個分）

「赤毛のアン」のお話のなかにも出てくるパンのようにやわらかいビスケット。

What you need：

2 cups	flour
1 tablespoon	baking powder
1/4 teaspoon	baking soda
1/2 teaspoon	salt
1/3 cup	shortening
3/4 cup	milk with 1 teaspoon vinegar in it (Let stand 5 minutes)

Stir flour, powder, soda and salt. Cut in shortening well. Make a well in the center and pour in milk.　Stir
until a ball forms.　Knead gently.　Pat or roll to 1cm thickness.　Cut with biscuit cutter.　Place on cookie
sheet.　Bake at 450℉, 10–12 minutes. Serve with butter, jam or honey.

American measures：1 teaspoon＝5cc　　　1 tablespoon＝15cc　　　1 cup＝16 tablespoons＝240cc
375℉＝190℃　　　450℉＝230℃

> 「準備は全部終わったわ、ダイアナ。あとは、明日の朝、私がレイヤーケーキを焼くのと、マリラがお茶の直前
> に、ベーキングパウダーを入れたビスケットを焼くだけよ。とにかくダイアナ、この二日間というもの、マリラ
> と二人、てんてこ舞いの忙しさだったのよ。牧師さんご一家をお茶に呼ぶって、大変なことだったのね……」
> 　　　　　　　　　　　　　　　　　　　　（「赤毛のアン」L.M. モンゴメリ、集英社 p.266 より引用）

排泄　　　連絡帳　　英文での
コミュニケーション

子どもが言う排泄に関する表現を学びましょう。また、英文を使って連絡帳のやりとりをする練習を
しましょう。

1. DOES ANYONE NEED TO GO POTTY?

排泄に関する表現を学びましょう。
真理先生がデイヴィーをトイレに誘います。

Mari ： Does anyone need to go potty?
Davy ： I want to go poo-poo.
Mari ： Follow me. The rest room is this way.

The rest room is this way.

Davy ： I'm finished. I made a big poop!
Mari ： Did you wipe your bottom?
Davy ： Yes, I did. I wiped.
Mari ： Did you wash your hands?
Davy ： Yes, I did. I washed.
Mari ： Did you flush the toilet?
Davy ： No, I didn't. I forgot!
Mari ： Uh-oh. You can't forget to flush.

英語ミニ知識　排泄に関係する子どもの表現

おしっこを表すことばには、pee, pee-pee, tee-tee, うんちを表すことばには、poo, poo-poo, poopなどがあります。
I have to pee ／ poo. I want to pee ／ poo. I want to go pee ／ poo. I have to go pee ／ go poo. などの表現例が
あります。おしっこに関しては、tinkle という言い方もあり、I have to tinkle などと言います。トイレを表す表現は、
rest room, bathroom などがありますが、本来、おまるを意味することば potty が、特に幼児にはトイレの意味で
使われます。Do you want to go to the potty? Do you need to go potty? などと言います。排泄の表現は、その家庭、
家庭で様々なようです。BM という表現を使う両親もいます。Do you have to have a BM? （うんちしたい？）とい
うように使います。BM は bowel movement の略、婉曲的な表現です。意味は便通、排便です。
〈その他の表現例〉
Let's take a potty break! Go potty. トイレ休憩よ。トイレ（おしっこ／うんち）へ行きなさい。
Can you pee-pee ／ poo-poo without help？ ／ Can you go by yourself？ ひとりでできる？
Did you pee-pee ／ poo-poo? Did you go pee-pee ／ poo-poo? おしっこ／うんちした？
Did you make a poop ／ have a BM? うんちした？

---

follow me 私について来て　　this way こちらへ　　wipe your bottom お尻を拭く　　flush the toilet トイレで水を流す

2. I WET MY PANTS.

デイヴィーが誤ってパンツを濡らしてしまいました

Davy： Mari-sensei, I wet my pants.

Mari： Don't worry, Davy. Here's some dry underwear.

You can put your wet underpants in this plastic bag.

Can you change by yourself?

Davy： Yes, I can. I can change by myself.

《PINWORM TEST》

日本の保育園などではぎょう虫卵検査が実施されていました。しかし、外国ではこの検査が一般的ではありません。真理先生がぎょう虫卵検査について説明しています。和訳してみましょう。

Mari-sensei explains to Jane as she shows her one of the test kits.

"The pinworm test collects an imprint of the child's anal area for microscopic examination. The worms live in the intestines and lay their eggs around the anus at night. They cause itching around the anus. Children catch worms through oral contact with contaminated objects or food. Often, members of a family are infested at the same time.

Testing procedure: First, take an imprint of the child's anus immediately after he wakes up in the morning, before he goes to the toilet. You do this on two separate mornings. On both sides of the clear plastic sheet there are "bull's eye" targets, one for each morning. On the first day, peel back the cellophane tape labeled number one, press the sticky side of the "bull's eye" firmly against the child's anal area and reseal it onto the plastic sheet. On the second day, with the tape on the opposite side, follow the same procedure. Return the test to school before the deadline. Parents will receive the results a week later. If your child has worms, please see a doctor. The doctor will treat the whole family together."

＊検査テープにはいくつかの種類があります。

保育ミニ知識　トイレットトレーニングについて

「うちの子、まだおむつがとれないのかしら？」と、同じ年頃の子どもたちのおむつが取れ始めるとお母さんたちは焦ってきます。しかし、排泄の自立に関しては、その子どものからだや精神的な発達などさまざまなことが影響しているために、かなり個人差があります。たとえば、からだの発達のことで言えば、一定の時間、一定の量のおしっこを膀胱に溜めておくことができるという機能が育っていなければ、排泄の自立をすることは不可能です。また、子どもによっては一時おむつが取れていたにもかかわらず、弟や妹が産まれたことで精神的に不安定になり、おむつに戻ってしまうというようなことも頻繁にあります。大人になってまでおむつをしている人はいないのですから、焦らずにその子どものペースで排泄の自立を促すというのが基本です。

---

wet my pants おもらしする(wet the bed おねしょする)　imprint（押してできた)印、跡、印影　anal 肛門の
microscopic 顕微鏡の　contaminate 汚染する　infest 寄生する　procedure 手順　bull's eye 標的の円

3. THE PARENT - TEACHER COMMUNICATION NOTEBOOK

連絡帳は保育者と保護者をつなぐための大切な役割を持っています。

これはジェーンさんと真理先生の連絡帳のやりとりです。

英文と日本文を読み比べてみて、英作文の作成のしかたを学びましょう。

Dear Mari-sensei,

Davy has diarrhea. It was probably from too much ice cream yesterday. He went to the bathroom 3 times this morning. He still has loose bowels. I gave him some medicine. He looks fine, and has an appetite. I just wanted to alert you to his condition. Please let him use the rest room when he needs to. Thank you.

Jane Smith

真理先生へ

デイヴィーはおなかを壊しています。昨日アイスクリームを食べすぎたようです。朝、3回もトイレに行きました。うんちがゆるいので、薬を飲ませました。元気はあり、食欲もありますが、このような様子であることをお知らせします。必要なときは、トイレに行かせるようにして下さい。よろしくお願いいたします。

ジェーン　スミス

Dear Jane,

Davy went to the rest room twice during lunchtime. He said he had a stomachache. He still seemed to suffer from diarrhea, but ate almost all his meal. I had him avoid milk. He didn't feel like having any snack, so I gave him only tea at snack time. He looked as cheerful as usual. He played tag today. I hope he gets better soon.

Mari Katayama

ジェーンさんへ

お昼ごはんを食べている途中におなかが痛いと言って2回トイレに行きました。下痢がまだ続いているようです。それでもお昼ご飯はほとんど食べました。ただし、牛乳だけは飲むのをやめさせました。おやつは食べたがらなかったので、お茶だけ飲ませました。いつものように元気はあります。今日は鬼ごっこをして遊びました。おなかの調子が早く良くなるといいですね。

片山真理

have diarrhea / have loose bowels / suffer from diarrhea 下痢する　　appetite 食欲　　almost all ほとんど全部　　feel like ～ing
～したい気がする　　get better 快方へ向かう

28

4. THE PARENT - TEACHER COMMUNICATION NOTEBOOK EXERCISE

英作文を完成する問題です。

真理先生は、からだの調子のこと、保育園での様子、連絡事項などジェーンさんに伝えます。下記の中から適当な単語を選んで空欄を埋めましょう。

surprised	larger	helping	fluids	extra	about	calling	fast
drew	irritated	bowel	one	returned	great	might	have

1. 今日、デイヴィーはお昼寝の後にうんちをしました。ちいさくて、かための便でした。水分を多めに取るように心がけてください。

   Today Davy had a _bowel_ movement after nap time. It was a small, hard stool. It is important to give him plenty of _____.

2. デイヴィーはお昼ごはんをお代わりしました。食欲が出てきたようで安心しました。

   Davy asked for another _____ at lunchtime. I am happy his appetite has _____.

3. 洋服の替えがなくなりました。明日持たせて下さい。

   Davy has no more _____ clothes. Please _____ Davy bring some tomorrow.

4. 友達の名前を覚えて呼ぶ姿が見られるようになりました。とても嬉しく思います。

   Davy started _____ his friends by their names. I think this is _____.

5. さつまいもの絵を書きました。とても大きな絵が描けました。

   Davy _____ a picture of a sweet potato. It was a very big _____.

6. 日本語の単語をずいぶん話すようになりました。とても嬉しいです。

   Now Davy has a _____ Japanese vocabulary. I am happy _____ this.

7. 今日は一日イライラしている様子でした。疲れが出ているのかもしれません。

   Davy was _____ all day today. He _____ have been tired.

8. 保育園でかけっこをしました。走るのが速いのでびっくりしました。

   The children ran a race. Davy really ran _____. I was _____!

＊便の表現例：硬い便 small, hard stools　　普通の便 normal stools　　軟らかい便 loose, watery stools

FIGHTING

けんか　文房具　体の部位　命令文

けんかや物の取り合いをしている子どもたちへの保育者の様々な言葉かけの表現を学びましょう。また、文房具や身体の部位に関する単語も学びましょう。

1. TAKASHI HIT MY HEAD.

デイヴィーとたかしのけんかに真理先生がかかわります。

Davy :	Ouch!
Mari :	What's the matter ?
Davy :	Takashi hit my head . (Pointing to the spot)
Mari :	Are you all right? Takashi, come here. Don't hit him .
Takashi :	I didn't mean to.
Mari :	Can you say, "I'm sorry" ?
Takashi :	I'm sorry.

 上の会話文に、身体の部位、行為などを表す語句を入れ替えて練習しましょう。

1. kicked my leg
   kick him

2. pinched my cheek
   pinch him

3. pushed my back
   push him

4. bit my left ear
   bite him

5. pulled my hair
   pull his hair

6. scratched my face
   scratch him

What's the matter ? どうしたの　　I didn't mean to. わざとじゃないよ

 ## 2. THAT'S A GOOD IDEA.

デイヴィーとたかしは物の取り合いでけんかになってしまいます。
真理先生がふたりの言い分を聞いています。

Davy ： That's my shovel . Give it back!

Mari ： Takashi, Davy wants the shovel . Let him use it .

Takashi ： I want it , too. I won't give it back. No, no, no, no.

Mari ： Well, what can we do ? Do you have any idea ?

Davy ： Yeah. Let's take turns.

Mari ： That's a good idea. Is it OK with you, Takashi ?

Takashi ： OK. But right now it's my turn.

上の会話文に文房具や遊具などを表す語句を入れ替えて練習しましょう。

1. That's / glue / it

2. Those are / scissors / them

3. Those are / crayons / them

4. Those are / blocks / them

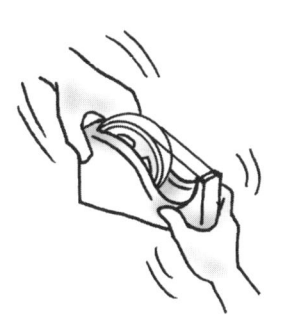

5. That's / Scotch tape / it

6. That's / stapler / it

take turns 順番にする　　glue のり

3. TAKASHI, COME HERE.

保育者が子どもに「○○してごらんなさい」と言うときには、肯定形の命令文（動詞の原形で始める）で表現できます。命令文+pleaseで、ややていねいな表現になり、命令文+will you?でさらに穏やかな表現になります。保育者が子どもにお手伝いを頼むとき Will you 〜？で「○○してくれる？」とていねいな依頼、軽い命令、勧誘を表現できます。

Mari ： Takashi, come here .
Mari ： Takashi, come here , please.
Mari ： Takashi, come here , will you ?
Mari ： Takashi, will you come here ?

上の会話文に下記の語句を入れ替えて練習しましょう。またストリーミングサイトでチャンツを聞き、リズムにのって繰り返し練習してみましょう。

Chanting exercise：

Be quiet ／ Be careful ／ Be still ／ Be nice

Turn on the light ／ Turn off the light ／ Go to sleep

Stop ／ Stop talking ／ Return to your seat

Raise your right hand ／ Raise your left hand ／ Raise your hands together

Watch out ／ Wait for me ／ Share the toys

Cut out the hearts ／ Color them pink ／ Glue them on the paper

Listen ／ Listen quietly ／ Listen to what I say

Open the drawer ／ Close the drawer ／ Get me a red marker

Give this letter to your mommy, please, will you?

Practice 形を表す英語表現を覚えましょう。

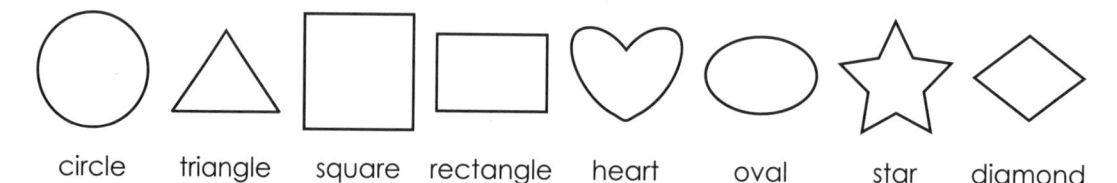

circle　triangle　square　rectangle　heart　oval　star　diamond

---

be still じっとしている（こどもの傷の手当てをしているときにも使える）　raise 上げる、高く揚げる

4. DON'T HIT HIM. DON'T DO THIS. DON'T DO THAT.

① 保育者が子どもに「○○しないで」と言うときは否定形の命令文（don't ＋動詞の原形）で表現できます。例文を読んで意味を理解しましょう。

1. **Don't put** your shoes here. Please take them to the shoe case.
2. Please pass the plate to me. **Don't drop** it.
3. **Don't grab** the rattle from the baby. You're a big boy, right?
4. **Don't cry**. You'll be all right. ／ It'll soon be over.
5. **Don't be** shy. Let's play together. Come on.
6. **Don't shout** at others. It's rude.
7. **Don't let** the children play by the river.

② 保育者が子どもにしてはいけないことを伝えます。
　 空欄に正しい語句を入れましょう。

run	noise	spill	touch	a mess	accept	play outside
open	~~play~~	jump		leave		fight with Takashi

1. Don't _____ play _____ with matches. They are not toys.
2. Here is your cookie and drink. Don't _____ the milk.
3. Don't _____ in the classroom. It's dangerous.
4. Don't _____ the heater.   It's very hot.
5. Don't _____ up and down on the bed. You may break it.
6. Don't _____ . We're all friends, right?
7. Don't _____ your toys here. The toy box is over there.
8. Don't make such _____ . Stop tapping your spoon, please?
9. Don't make _____ . It's time to clean up.
10. Don't _____ your door to strangers.
11. Don't _____ presents from strangers.
12. Don't _____ today. It's raining.

---

grab 横取りする　　Don't be shy. 恥ずかしがらないで　　others ほかの人たち　　rude 無作法な、失礼な

5. LET HIM USE IT. LET'S TAKE TURNS.

① 「私（たち）に○○させて」と1人称に対する命令文の場合、let＋目的語（me／us）＋動詞の原形を使います。例文を読み、下記の和文を英訳しましょう。

・Let me help you.	手伝わせて。
・Let me have a look.	見せて。
・Let me read you a story.	お話を読みましょう。
・Let me sit next to you.	隣に座らせて。

・Let me _____.　　　　私も仲間にいれて。

② 「誰々に○○させてあげて」と3人称に対する命令文の場合、let＋目的語＋動詞の原形を使います。例文を読み、下記の和文を英訳しましょう。

・Let Davy do it first.	先にデイヴィーにやらせてあげて。
・Let Takashi go.	たかしを放して。行かせてあげて。
・Let the children play indoors.	子どもたちを室内で遊ばせましょう。
・Let the parents know about the field trip.	ご父兄に遠足のことを知らせましょう。

・Let Davy _____ the bicycle.　　デイヴィーに自転車を貸してあげて。

③ 「みんなで○○しよう」と提案・勧誘を表わすとき、Let's＋動詞の原形を使います。例文を読み、下記の和文を英訳しましょう。

・Let's play a game.	ゲームをしましょう。
・Let's get in a line.	一列に並びましょう。
・Let's walk slowly.	ゆっくり歩きましょう。
・Let's make a big circle.	大きな円をつくりましょう。
・Let's clap hands three times.	3回、手をたたきましょう。
・Let's pretend we're elephants.	ぞうさんになりましょう。
・Let's pretend to be ants.	ありさんになりましょう。

・Let's _____.　　　　お片づけしましょう。

---

pretend (that) 節 / to do　ふりをする

6. MY FACE AND BODY

ここでは身体の部位に関する単語を学びましょう。絵を見て、空欄に番号を入れましょう。

__head __back __stomach __chest __shoulder __neck __ear __eye

__eyebrow __cheek __nose __mouth __leg __foot __toe __knee

__calf __ankle __thigh __arm __hand __elbow __wrist __finger

__bellybutton __bottom __forehead

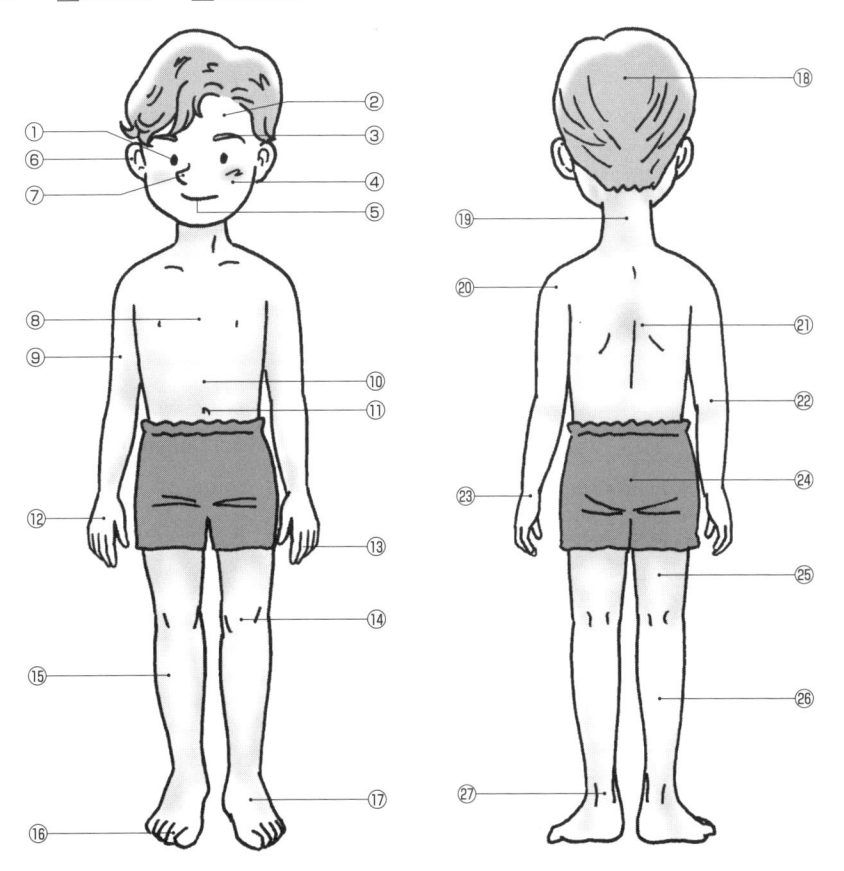

HEAD, SHOULDERS, KNEES AND TOES

Point to body parts as you sing.

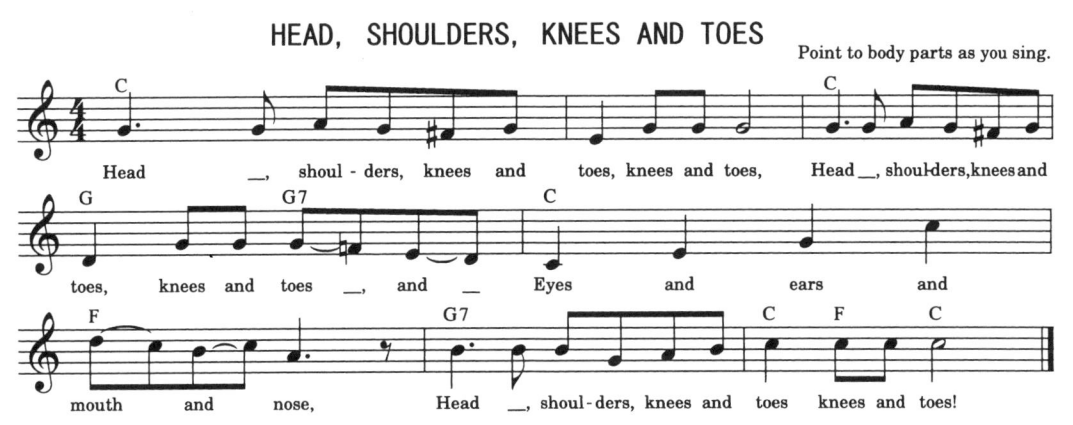

Head __, shoul-ders, knees and toes, knees and toes, Head __, shoul-ders, knees and

toes, knees and toes __, and __ Eyes and ears and

mouth and nose, Head __, shoul-ders, knees and toes knees and toes!

INJURIES AND ILLNESSES

# Unit 11

けが・病気　症状　医療機関　救急処置

デイヴィーが保育園でけがや病気になったことをジェーンさんに伝えます。けがや病気に関する表現を学びましょう。また、医療機関や救急処置に関する語句も学びましょう。

1. WHAT'S THE MATTER?

真理先生は、デイヴィーがけがしたことをジェーンさんに伝えます。

Jane： What's the matter?
Mari： Davy fell down and scraped his knee.

 上の会話文にけがをした部位やけがの状態を表す語句を入れ替えて練習しましょう。

1. hit his leg against a chair and got a bruise.

2. got his finger caught in the door, and it's swollen.

3. hit his forehead against a wall and got a bump.

4. used scissors and cut his hand.

5. played soccer, and the ball hit his shoulder.

6. played in tall grass and got a rash on his hands.

7. was bitten by an insect on the arm and got a welt.

---

cf. p.64　　fall down ころぶ　　get his finger caught in the door ドアに指を挟む　　get(have)＋目的語＋過去分詞〜されるという被害の意味を表す経験受動態　getの方が口語的　　be swollen 腫れている　　be bitten by 〜にかまれる　　insect(bug) 昆虫　　welt みみずばれ

2. I'M REALLY SORRY FOR WHAT HAPPENED TODAY.

デイヴィーは友達とけんかをしてケガをしてしまいました。真理先生はけがの状態と処置をジェーンさんに伝えます。

Mari： Jane, Davy had a fight with Moe and got his face scratched.
Jane： Oh, no.
Mari： I disinfected the cuts. I'm really sorry for what happened today.
Jane： I'm just glad it's not worse.
Mari： I'll keep a closer watch on the children.

 上の会話文に、けがをした状態や処置を表す語句を入れ替えて練習しましょう。

1. had a fight with Takashi and got his arm bitten.
   covered the teethmarks with a Band-Aid.

2. tripped over a stone and sprained his ankle.
   put an ice pack over the injured area.

3. missed a step, fell down, and cut his knee.
   washed the cut, and the bleeding stopped quickly.

4. spilled soup and burned his toes.
   cooled the burned area under cold running water.

5. played in the sun too long and had a bloody nose.
   had him sit still for a while.

6. was chasing bees and got stung.
   removed the stinger.

7. walked with bare feet and got a splinter in his foot.
   got it out.

---

cf. p.64　get his face scratched 顔をひっかかれる　disinfect 消毒する　I'm just glad it's not worse ひどくならなくてよかった　keep a closer watch より注意する　teethmarks 歯型　trip over つまずく　miss a step 踏み外す　bleeding 出血　get stung 刺される　stinger（昆虫の）針　remove 取り除く　bare feet 裸足　splinter とげ

3. MY TUMMY HURTS.

デイヴィーは真理先生にお腹が痛いと訴えてきました。

Mari ： What's the matter with you?
You aren't eating at all .
Davy ： My tummy hurts .
Mari ： Your tummy hurts ? Let me see.
I'll take your temperature.

 上の会話文に、子どもの状態や病気の症状などを
表す語句を入れ替えて練習しましょう。

1. You look pale ／ I have a headache ／ You have a headache

2. You're shaking ／ I have chills ／ You have chills

3. Your cheeks are flushed and your eyes are dull ／ I feel sick ／ You feel sick

4. You 're sneezing and coughing ／ I feel hot ／ You feel hot

5. You're rubbing your ear ／ I have an earache ／ You have an earache

6. You aren't drinking your milk ／ I have a sore throat ／ You have a sore throat

7. You look drowsy ／ My nose is running ／ Your nose is running

8. You're scratching your head ／ My head is itchy ／ Your head is itchy

---

cf. p.64　　look pale 顔色が悪い　　eyes are dull 目がどろんとしている(元気がない)　　feel sick 気分・気持ちが悪い
rub 擦る　　drowsy うとうとしている、眠たい　　nose is running 鼻(水)が出る　　itchy 痒い

4. IF YOU ARE CONCERNED ABOUT HIM, CONSULT THE DOCTOR.

真理先生はジェーンさんにデイヴィーの体調を伝え、お医者さんに行くことを薦めます。

Mari： Jane, Davy is coughing and has a runny nose .

Jane： Really?

Mari： He may have a cold .

Jane： What should I do?

Mari： If you are concerned about him, consult the doctor.

上の会話文に体調や病名を表す語句を入れ替えて練習しましょう。

1. Davy has a headache and a fever ／ have the flu

2. Davy's eyes have a thick discharge ／ have conjunctivitis

3. Davy has an earache ／ have an ear infection

4. Davy feels itchy ／ have impetigo

5. Davy has a toothache ／ have a cavity

6. Davy's head is itchy ／ have head lice

7. Davy has an upset stomach ／ have a stomach flu

お医者さんなど医療関係者名の和訳の記号を書き入れましょう。

1. pediatrician ___c___	a. 歯科医
2. surgeon _____	b. 保健婦
3. druggist _____	c. 小児科医
4. nurse _____	d. 看護師
5. eye doctor _____	e. 内科医
6. ear, nose and throat (ENT) doctor _____	f. 薬剤師
7. school nurse _____	g. 保健の先生
8. dermatologist (skin specialist) _____	h. 産科医
9. dentist _____	i. 耳鼻咽喉科医
10. physician _____	j. 眼科医
11. (public) health nurse _____	k. 外科医
12. obstetrician _____	l. 皮膚科医

---

cf. p.64　If you are concerned about him, consult the doctor ご心配なら、お医者さんに相談してください。　discharge 排出（流出）物、分泌物　ここでは目やにの意　ear infection（外耳炎、内耳炎などの）耳の炎症　head lice 頭ジラミ　an upset stomach 不調な胃腸　stomach flu 吐き気、下痢など胃腸の不調を伴う感冒

5. COMMON CHILDHOOD INJURIES, ILLNESSES AND SYMPTOMS

よく使われるけがや病気の病状を表す英語表現です。
ストリーミングサイトで音声を聞いて発音練習をしましょう。

be sick ／ be ill　病気になる

be injured ／ be hurt　けがをする

have a cold　風邪をひく

have a fever　熱がある

have chills　悪寒がする

have a headache　頭痛がする

have a stomachache　腹痛がする

have diarrhea　下痢をする

have no appetite　食欲がない

have a sore throat　喉が痛い

have an earache　耳が痛い

have sore eyes　目が痛い

have a runny nose　鼻水が出る

have a stuffy nose　鼻が詰まる

have a bloody nose　鼻血が出る

have a rash　発疹(吹き出もの)がでる

have an insect bite　虫にかまれる

have a sunburn　(赤くなり痛い)日焼けをする

have a toothache　歯痛がする

have a cavity　虫歯がある

have a broken tooth　歯が折れている

have hiccups　しゃっくりが出る

have pinworms　寄生虫がいる

have an allergic reaction　アレルギー反応が出る

cough　咳をする

sneeze　くしゃみをする

vomit ／ throw up　吐く

feel dizzy　目がまわる、ふらふらする

hurt one's knee　膝を痛める

cut one's arm　腕を切る

scratch one's face　顔に引っ掻き傷をする

burn one's finger　指をやけどする

bruise one's back　背中にあざができる

break one's leg　足(の骨)を折る

twist one's wrist　手首をひねる

scrape one's elbow　ひじを擦りむく

sprain one's ankle　足首をくじく

fall from a ladder　梯子から落ちる

bleed　出血する

drown　溺れる

choke　詰まらせる、窒息する

swallow objects ／ poisons　誤飲する

get an electric shock　感電する

get frostbite　しもやけになる

以下の単語は名詞でも使われます。

cut　切り傷

scratch　すり傷、かき傷

burn　やけど

bruise　あざ、打ち身

英語ミニ知識　子どもの病気・病名　**Children's diseases**

はしか　measles	インフルエンザ　influenza	とびひ　impetigo
風疹　rubella (German measles)	アトピー性皮膚炎　atopic eczema	結膜炎　conjunctivitis
水ぼうそう　chicken pox	あせも　heat rash	中耳炎　otitis media
百日咳　whooping cough	湿疹　eczema	ぜんそく　asthma
おたふく風邪　mumps	おむつかぶれ　diaper rash	ひきつけ　convulsion
破傷風　tetanus (lockjaw)	水いぼ　molluscum contagiosum	川崎病　Kawasaki disease
手足口病　hand-foot-and-mouth disease	乳児突然死症候群　sudden infant death syndrome (SIDS)	

6. FIRST AID AND MEDICAL CARE

救急処置に関する語句を学びましょう。絵を見て、単語の空欄に番号を入れましょう。

___Band-Aid   ___adhesive tape   ___bandage   ___ointment   ___gauze   ___ice pack

___chemical cold pack   ___tweezers   ___cotton balls   ___tablet   ___pill   ___capsule

___cough syrup   ___cough drops   ___throat lozenges   ___nasal spray   ___eye drops

___eye chart   ___wheelchair   ___crutch   ___thermometer   ___scale   ___ambulance

___patient   ___health insurance certificate   ___cast   ___nurse

---

英語ミニ知識 医療に関する表現 **Medical treatment**

手に包帯を巻く bandage a hand   軟膏を塗る apply／put on ointment   レントゲンを撮る take an X-ray

子どもを医者に連れていく take a child to the doctor   診察を受ける see／consult a doctor

救急車を呼ぶ call an ambulance   入院する be hospitalized   ギブスをはめる wear a cast

心肺蘇生法 CPR（cardiopulmonary resuscitation）

---

chemical cold pack 湿布（chemical hot pack 温湿布）   tablet 錠剤   pill 丸薬   health insurance certificate 保険証

 Unit 12

電話での応対　園行事への招待　メッセージを書く　リスニング

ジェーンさんから保育園に電話がありました。電話での応対や電話で受けた連絡をメッセージに書いて伝えるという練習をしましょう。

1. HELLO. THIS IS MINATO NURSERY SCHOOL.

谷園長はジェーンさんからデイヴィーの
欠席の連絡を受けます。

Mrs. Tani：	Hello. This is Minato Nursery School.
Jane：	Hello. This is Jane Smith speaking.
Mrs. Tani：	Good morning, Jane. May I help you?
Jane：	Davy will be absent from school today. His temperature has been 101℉ since last night.
Mrs. Tani：	That's too bad. I hope he gets better soon.
Jane：	Thank you. Bye.

Practice　体温（熱）の聞き方と答え方

A：What's your temperature?　　B：It's 101℉. (one hundred one degrees Fahrenheit)

A：What's your temperature?　　B：It's 39.8℃. (thirty-nine point eight degrees centigrade [Celsius])

英語ミニ知識　摂氏と華氏、度量衡換算について ───────

　日本では、一般的に熱があるという状態は摂氏（centigrade）37℃以上の体温をさします。アメリカでは温度、体温を表すのに華氏（Fahrenheit）が使われ、98.6℉までが平熱とされています。摂氏と華氏の換算は、次のとおりです。centigrade [Celsius]=$\frac{5}{9}$（Fahrenheit－32）Fahrenheit=$\frac{9}{5}$ centigrade + 32　Davyの華氏101度を摂氏に換算すると熱は何度出たのでしょうか。計算してみましょう。また、98.6℉も換算してみましょう。
このほかにも、アメリカでは長さを inch(in.)、foot(ft.)、yard(yd.)、mile(mi.)、重さを ounce(oz.)、pound(lb.)、容積を pint(pt.)、quart(qt.) という度量で表すことが一般的です。

長さ	1 mile=1760 yards　　1 yard=3 feet=0.9144m　　1 foot=12 inches=0.3048m　　1 inch=2.54cm
重さ	1 pound=16 ounces　　1 pound=0.4536kg　　1 ounce=0.0283495kg
容積	1/4 gallon=1 quart=2 pints=0.946 liter　　1 pint=16 fluid ounces　　1 fluid ounce=29.573 ml

---

hello もしもし　　this is ～ speaking こちら～です　　be absent from school 学校を休む

2. MAY I TAKE A MESSAGE?

谷園長はジェーンさんから電話でデイヴィーの欠席の連絡を受け、テレフォンメッセージに必要なことを書き入れました。

Mrs. Tani：	Hello. This is Minato Nursery School.
Jane：	Hello. This is Jane Smith speaking. May I speak to Mari-sensei?
Mrs. Tani：	Oh, she hasn't come in yet. May I take a message?
Jane：	Yes, please. My mother will be arriving at Narita Airport today.
	Davy and I will pick her up, so Davy will be absent today.
Mrs. Tani：	I hope your mother will have a great time here.
Jane：	Thank you. Bye.

TELEPHONE MESSAGE

Date: September 8   **Time**: 7：45 a.m.

Please call back.   Yes ☐   No ☑

For: Mari-sensei

From: Jane Smith

Phone:

Message: Davy will be absent today .   Jane and Davy will pick up
Davy's grandmother at Narita Airport.

Signed: A.Tani

Practice 数字（序数）の読み方を練習しましょう。

1st first   2nd second   3rd third   4th fourth   5th fifth   6th sixth   7th seventh   8th eighth   9th ninth   10th tenth   11th eleventh   12th twelfth   13th thirteenth   14th fourteenth   15th fifteenth   16th sixteenth   17th seventeenth   18th eighteenth   19th nineteenth   20th twentieth   21st twenty-first   22nd twenty-second   23rd twenty-third   24th twenty-fourth   25th twenty-fifth   26th twenty-sixth   27th twenty-seventh   28th twenty-eighth   29th twenty-ninth   30th thirtieth   31st thirty-first

3. MAY I SPEAK TO MRS. SMITH?

電話の応対の練習をしましょう。
真理先生とジェーンさんの電話の
やりとりです。

Hello. This is Mari katayama. May I speak to Mrs. Smith?

Speaking.

① 真理先生はデイヴィーの急病を伝えます。

Mari： Jane, I'm sorry to bother you at the office, but Davy has a slight fever and blisters on the inside of the mouth.

Jane： Oh, my. It sounds like hand-foot-and-mouth disease.

Mari： Could you come to pick him up right away?

Jane： Of course, I will. I think I can get there in an hour. Thank you for calling. See you soon.

② 真理先生は参観日に出席してもらいたいと伝えます。

Mari： Jane, next Monday we'll have a parents' observation day. All the parents are invited to their children's classes.

Jane： Oh, really?

Mari： I hope you and your husband can come. Do you think you can?

Jane： Of course, we'd love to. Thank you for calling. We're looking forward to the observation day. Good night.

③ 真理先生はお誕生会に参加してもらいたいと伝えます。

Mari： Jane, next Wednesday we'll have a birthday party for Davy and other children who were born in November. All the parents are invited to the party.

Jane： Oh, really?

Mari： I hope you and your husband can come. Do you think you can?

Jane： We'd love to, but we have another appointment. I'm very sorry. Thank you for calling. I'm sure Davy will have a lot of fun even though we can't come.

Mari： Yes, I think he will. Don't worry. Good-bye.

I'm sorry to bother you at the office お仕事中にお邪魔してすみません。　slight fever 微熱　blister 水疱　in an hour 一時間後　parents' observation day 参観日　have another appointment 他に予定がある

41

4. TELEPHONE MESSAGES

ストリーミングサイトで音声を聞いてテレフォンメッセージに必要なことを書き入れ
てみましょう。

1.TELEPHONE MESSAGE

Date：_____   **Time**：_____

Please call back.   Yes ☐   No ☐

For：_____

From：_____

Phone：_____

Message：_____

_____

Signed：_____

2.TELEPHONE MESSAGE

Date：_____   **Time**：_____

Please call back.   Yes ☐   No ☐

For：_____

From：_____

Phone：_____

Message：_____

_____

Signed：_____

3.TELEPHONE MESSAGE

Date：_____   **Time**：_____

Please call back.   Yes ☐   No ☐

For：_____

From：_____

Phone：_____

Message：_____

_____

Signed：_____

FIELD TRIP

 遠足　交通機関　 if　園からのお知らせ

遠足に行くことをジェーンさんに伝えます。遠足に行く場所や交通手段を伝える表現を学びましょう。
また、ifを使った仮定形を練習したり、保育園の年間行事を示す表現も学びましょう。

1. WE'RE GOING TO THE ZOO NEXT FRIDAY.

真理先生はジェーンさんに遠足へ行くことを伝えます。

Mari ： We're going to the zoo next Friday.

Jane ： Really? That sounds fun.

Mari ： This is a school letter that tells
you what time and where we'll
meet, and the things we'll need.

Jane ： How will we get to the zoo ?

Mari ： We'll take a train .

上の会話文に場所や交通手段を表す
語句を入れ替えて練習しましょう。

1. the park ／ take a bus

2. the aquarium ／ take a ferry

3. the amusement park ／ walk

4. the art museum ／ take the subway

5. the puppet show ／ take the monorail

6. the farm ／ take a chartered bus

英語ミニ知識 交通手段の表現

take a train / bus / taxi / ferry = go by train / bus / taxi / ferry

take the subway / monorail = go by subway / monorail

walk = go on foot　go by bicycle / bike / motorcycle = go on a bicycle / bike / motorcycle

---

How will we get to the zoo? どのように動物園には行くのですか。　　aquarium 水族館　　amusement park 遊園地　　art
museum 美術館　　subway 地下鉄　　puppet show 人形劇　　farm 農場、農園　　chartered bus 貸切バス

2. IF IT RAINS, WE WILL POSTPONE THE FIELD TRIP.

真理先生はジェーンさんに、雨が降った場合には遠足が延期になることを伝えます。

Mari ： We're going on a field trip tomorrow.

Jane ： OK. Where do we meet?

Mari ： At the south exit of Minato station.

Jane ： If it rains, what will we do?

Mari ： If it rains, we will postpone the field trip.
A decision will be made by 6 o'clock
in the morning. Parents will be called.

Jane ： OK. So, if there is no field trip, we'll
just come to nursery school as usual?

Mari ： That's right.

英語ミニ知識 子どもたちに大人気のマザーグースとは？ ────

マザーグース（Mother Goose）あるいは、ナスリーライム（Nursery Rhymes）と描かれている本や絵本を手にとって開いたことはありますか？それは、英米国の子どもたちに愛されている童謡、遊び唄、手遊び唄、なぞなぞ、詩などの伝承童話集です。これら多くの唄や詩、格言を子どもたちは小さいころから口ずさみ、成長しています。雨に因んだかわいらしい唄をひとつご紹介しましょう。小さな子どもの気持ちが伝わってきませんか。

保育者はこの歌のJohnnyのところを担当の子どもたちの名前に替えて歌うようにします。自分の名前で歌われると、子どもたちはとても喜びます。

RAIN, RAIN, GO AWAY

C

Rain, rain go a - way. Come a - gain a - noth - er day.

G7　　　　　　　　　　　　　C

Lit - tle John - ny wants to play. - Rain, __ rain, __ go - a - way.

---

exit 出口　　postpone 延期する　　decision 決定

3. DEAR PARENTS

みなと保育園からジェーンさんに遠足に関するお知らせが渡されました。
日本語に訳してみましょう。

Minato Nursery School

November 15, xxxx

Dear parents,

The children are enjoying the beautiful fall days of November and are having a good time playing with their friends. This letter is to notify you about our field trip for 5-year-old children. We are going to the zoo to enjoy the different animals.

Date:	*Friday, November 22nd*
Meeting place:	*The south exit of Minato station*
Meeting time:	*9:00 a.m.*
Things to bring:	*Lunch, thermos, picnic blanket, wet towel, snacks, raincoat or umbrella, change of clothes*
Dress code:	*Children should dress in casual, comfortable clothing. No sandals are allowed.*

The field trip will be postponed if it rains. A decision will be made by 6 o'clock in the morning. In case of postponement, we will contact parents through the school's phone tree.

Please be sure to come to the station by 9:00 a.m. Do not come to school. We will go to the zoo by train. We hope everyone will come.

---

notify 知らせる　　picnic blanket レジャーシート　　dress code 服装のきまり　　casual, comfortable clothing カジュアルで動きやすい服装　　allow 許す、認める　　in case of 〜の場合は　　postponement 延期　　contact 連絡する　　phone tree 電話の連絡網リスト

4. ANNUAL SCHOOL CALENDAR

みなと保育園の年間行事予定表です。保育園にどのような行事があるのか理解しましょう。
日本の伝統行事に関する表現も覚えましょう。

Four seasons： **Spring, Summer, Fall, Winter**

April

entrance ceremony
health checkups

May

Children's Day
Mother's Day

June

Father's Day
parents' observation day
dental checkups

July

Tanabata （Star Festival）
first day of swimming class

August

summer festival

September

Respect-for-the-Aged Day
fire drill
moon viewing

October

Sports Day

November

field trip
potato digging day

December

year-end party
concert

January

New Year's party

February

Setsubun （the day before
the beginning of spring）
exhibition

March

Hinamatsuri
（Doll Festival）
graduation ceremony

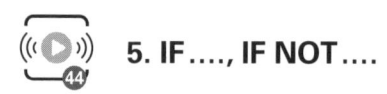

5. IF...., IF NOT....

条件文ifを使った文章を読み、ifの使い方と助動詞（will, can, may）を使った表現を学びましょう。みなと保育園でパートの保育助手をしているやよいさんへの、お母さんからのメッセージです。

Yayoi is a part-time assistant at the nursery school and also is a college student. Her major is Early Childhood Education. She studies in the daytime and works after school.

Yayoi's mother says:

If you get up early, you will have more time in the morning.

If you have more time in the morning, you can have breakfast.

If you have breakfast, you won't be hungry in class.

If you are not hungry, you can concentrate on your work.

If you concentrate on your work, you can take more notes.

If you take more notes, you can learn more English words.

If you learn more English words, you will improve your English.

If you improve your English, you will pass the test.

If you pass the test, you may get an A.

If you get an A, your father and I will be very happy.

Yayoi's mother continues:

If you don't go to bed early, you won't get up early.

If you don't get up early, you will skip breakfast.

If you skip breakfast, you may be hungry in class.

If you feel hungry in class, you can't concentrate on your work.

If you don't concentrate on your work, you won't take notes.

If you don't take notes, you can't learn English words.

If you don't learn English words, you can't improve your English.

If you don't improve your English, you may fail the test.

If you fail the test, you may get an F.

If you get an F, your father and I will get very angry.

So, will you go to bed earlier today or not?

---

concentrate on ～に集中する　improve 上達させる　fail a test 試験に落ちる　an A=excellent 優（秀）　an F=Failure 不可（落第点）

6. MARI–SENSEI TALKS ABOUT SAFETY AND WEATHER.

① 真理先生は安全に気をつけて、子どもたちに注意をうながします。
意味が合うように2つの文を線で結びましょう。

1. You'll burn your skin,   ·   · if you play on a wet, slippery floor.

2. You'll stumble and fall,   ·   · if you touch a hot iron.

3. You'll get an electric shock, ·   · if you play with a knife.

4. You'll cut yourself,   ·   · if you play on the stairs.

5. You'll fall down,   ·   · if you put your fingers in electric sockets.

② 真理先生は天気にあわせて、明日の予定を子どもたちに話します。
意味が合うように2つの文を線で結びましょう。

1. We'll play in the wading pool,   ·   · if it's raining again.

2. We'll build a snowman,   ·   · if it's hot.

3. We'll take a walk in the park,   ·   · if it's sunny.

4. We'll play indoors,   ·   · if it's very cold.

5. We'll make a Teruterubozu paper doll, ·   · if it's snowing.

7. TRANSPORTATION

陸上、水上、空のカテゴリーに、下記の乗り物を分類して、番号を書き入れましょう。

1. car	2. ferry	3. train	4. jet	5. ship	6. canoe
7. sailboat	8. local bus	9. raft	10. subway	11. yacht	12. taxi/cab
13. airplane	14. mountain bike	15. helicopter	16. truck		

Land	Air	Water

＊ Teruterubozu is a small paper doll hung out the window as a wish for good weather

赤ちゃんへの　　　育児用品　　　赤ちゃんの
　言葉かけ　　　　　　　　　　　　成長・発達

デイヴィーの妹のキャロラインが誕生し、０歳児クラスに入園しました。赤ちゃんへの言葉かけを学びましょう。また、育児用品や赤ちゃんの成長・発達を表す表現も学びましょう。

1. THIS MUST BE DAVY'S BABY SISTER.

キャロラインの担任のきよ子先生と
ジェーンさんが話しています。

Kiyoko：	Hello, Jane. This must be Davy's baby sister, Caroline. What should I call her?
Jane：	Please call her Carrie.
Kiyoko：	How old is she?
Jane：	She is 57 days old, almost two months old.

Kiyoko：	What's wrong, Carrie? Why are you crying?
Jane：	She might be wet or hungry.
Kiyoko：	Let's take a look. The diaper is OK . I'll feed you right now.
Jane：	Peek-a-boo. Don't cry, Carrie. The milk is coming.
Kiyoko：	There! She's drinking a lot.

上の会話文に次の語句を入れ替えて
練習しましょう。

wet ／ change it ／ diaper ／ smiling

```
— Caroline Smith —
Born： Dec 8, 20XX
Weight： 6 lbs. 14ozs.
Length： 23 ins.
```

英語ミニ知識　おむつと授乳

　おむつはアメリカ英語でdiaper、イギリス英語ではnappyです。紙おむつ disposable diaper　布おむつ cloth diaper　汚れたおむつ wet/soiled diaper　おむつカバー diaper cover　おむつかぶれ diaper rash　おむつをする put a diaper on a baby/diaper a baby　おむつを取りかえる change the baby's diaper/change the baby　などの表現があります。授乳するはnurse a babyや feed a babyです。母乳を意味する場合、breast-feed a baby, 人工乳の場合 bottle-feed a baby などの表現があります。乳児用の人工乳はformulaと言います。哺乳瓶はfeeding/ nursing/ baby bottle といろいろな呼び方があります。哺乳瓶の乳首はnipple, イギリス英語ではteatです。

What's wrong? どうしたの？　　there ほら

2. BABY'S ROOM

育児用品に関する単語を覚えましょう。
キャロラインの部屋の絵を見て、単語の __欄に該当する番号を入れましょう。

__crib __mobile __diaper cover __disposable diaper __baby wipes __bib __baby bottle __training pants __teething ring __formula __pacifier __rattle __stroller __baby carriage __cradle __baby powder __cloth diaper __diaper rash cream __diaper pail __high chair __diaper pins __walker __potty __changing table __baby monitor __stuffed animal __cotton swab

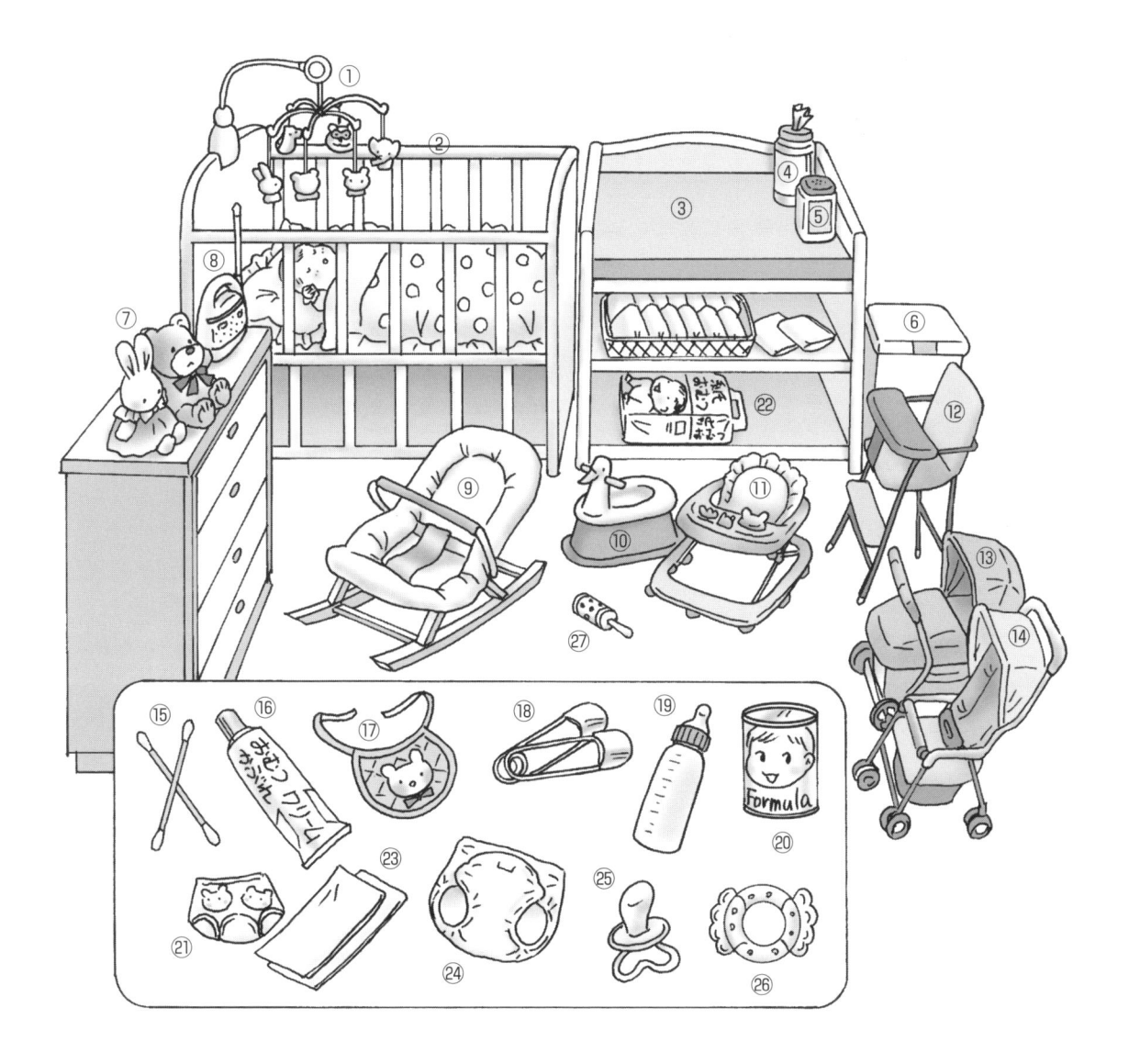

3. WHAT DO BABIES DO? HOW DO CHILDREN GROW?

赤ちゃんの成長を英語で追ってみましょう。保育の知識を生かしながら和訳してみましょう。

（赤ちゃんの成長は個人差が非常に大きいものです。記入されている月数は、およそのものです。）

Birth	cry
	sleep
	nurse / drink breast milk
	drink formula / drink bottle milk
	burp
	be startled by loud sounds
	smile
	wriggle
	turn towards a voice
3 months	hold their heads up
	drool
	kick
5 months	roll over
	cut first teeth
	play with their feet

7 months   sit unsupported

reach out for a rattle

8 months   crawl

tap the table with a spoon or toys

throw their dinner

play peek-a-boo

wave bye-bye

10 months walk holding onto furniture

poke

open drawers and pull things out

11 months stand alone

13 months walk

say "mama"

15 months drink from a cup

4. MOTHER AND CHILD HEALTH HANDBOOK

キャロラインの母子手帳の内容です。前ページの赤ちゃんの成長の過程を参考にキャロラインの成長のおよその月数を記入してみましょう。

名前　Infant's name Caroline Smith	出生体重　Weight 3110 g	出生身長　Height 58 cm	妊娠週数 (Duration of pregnancy) 40 weeks

栄養の種類	□母乳栄養	□人工乳栄養	☑混合栄養	
Feeding	Breast milk	Formula milk	Mixed	

①首のすわり（Lifts head） 　3 months old	⑤はいはい（Crawls） 　__ months old
②歯の生え始め（Cuts first teeth） 　__ months old	⑥つかまり立ち（Stands with support） 　__ months old
③寝返り（Rolls over） 　__ months old	⑦一人歩き（Walks） 　__ months old
④一人座り（Sits without support） 　__ months old	⑧話し始め（Says simple words） 　__ months old

予防接種（Vaccination）	接種年月日　Immunization date
BCG　　　　（B.C.G.）	（　　　/　　　/　　　）
ポリオ　　　（Polio）	（　　　/　　　/　　　）
麻疹　　　　（Measles）	（　　　/　　　/　　　）
三種混合（ジフテリア、百日咳、破傷風） 　　　　　（DPT）（Diphtheria, Pertussis and Tetanus combined）	（　　　/　　　/　　　）

───（保育ミニ知識）　アメリカと日本の赤ちゃんへの接し方に関する文化的な違い ───

　日本の育児では、スキンシップが大切であると言われ、おんぶや抱っこを頻繁にし、夜寝るときも同じ布団で添い寝をしたりします。しかし、アメリカではスキンシップは大切にしながらも、それ以上に子どもは一人の人格を備えた人間であるということを大切にします。そのため、生まれる前から赤ちゃん専用の部屋が用意され、誕生後間もなくから自分の部屋で寝ます。夜泣きをしても、よほどのことがなければ親がとんでくるなどということはありません。それは、独りで過ごすという時間は自分と向き合うための大事な時間であると考えられているからです。

　アメリカと日本の赤ちゃんへの接し方の違いには、育児に対する考え方（育児観）の違いがみられます。そのどちらが良くてどちらが悪いかなどと決めることはできませんし、決めようとすること自体無意味です。なぜならば、育児観とはその国や民族の生活様式や価値観、人間観など様々なものが、時代や社会のあり方によって変化しながら受け継がれてきたものだからです。アメリカと日本では赤ちゃんへの接し方が異なるかもしれませんが、いずれにしても親が精一杯の愛情をかけて子育てしていることに変わりはありません。アメリカでは、baby monitor を赤ちゃんのベッド脇に置いて利用するお母さんやお父さんが少なくありません。生まれたときから親と離れて寝ているために、赤ちゃんの様子や泣き声を察知するための欠かせない装置なのです。

5. A LETTER FROM DR. TANAKA, JANE'S OBSTETRICIAN

産婦人科医師の田中博士からジェーンさんに新生児の育て方に関する手紙がきました。

Dear Mrs. Smith,

Congratulations on the birth of your daughter, Caroline. I'd like to give you some general advice for taking care of a newborn baby.

1. Infants usually know how much milk they need, so you can feed her as much as she wants when she is hungry. If she is not getting enough, she will probably cry. In the early weeks, mothers usually feed their babies every two or three hours. All babies swallow some air while they are drinking their milk. After nursing, you need to burp her.

2. Most babies have several bowel movements a day. The stools are usually of a light-yellow color. If they are black, red, chalk white, or if you see blood in them, you should contact the doctor.

3. Babies usually cannot control their body temperature well, so you should keep their rooms at an even temperature (65°-68°F). You should be careful not to dress her too heavily or lightly.

4. Also, babies are not immune to germs. You should not keep her outside for a long time, especially in places where there are many people. I recommend sunbaths for babies. You can take her outdoors for fresh air, particularly when it is nice and sunny. As for bathing, you should bathe her once a day.

Sincerely,

n. Tanaka

---

congratulations おめでとう　　every two or three hours 2,3時間ごとに　　swallow 飲み込む　　even temperature 一定の温度
immune 免疫力がある　　germ 細菌、病原菌　　sunbath 日なたぼっこ、日光浴　　take ～outdoors for fresh air 外気浴させる
bathe 沐浴させる

GRADUATION DAY

Unit 15

卒園　祝福・感謝　記念日　ファミリーツリー　クロスワードパズル

デイヴィーの卒園式です。祝福や感謝の表現を学びましょう。また、記念日や家族を表す表現も学びましょう。

1. DAVY, CONGRATULATIONS!

真理先生がデイヴィーを祝福しています。

Mari : Davy, congratulations! You finished
　　　　 nursery school. I'll miss you.
　　　　 I have a present for you. Here you are.
Davy : Wow! May I open it?
Mari : Go ahead. I hope you like it.
Davy : D-i-p-l-o-m-a. Diploma. You made this? Thank you.
Mari : You're welcome. Well, it's hard to say good-bye
　　　　 now. Come back anytime. OK?
Davy : Thank you. Sayonara, Mari-sensei.

真理先生はデイヴィーのために英語の卒園証書を作りました。アメリカの保育園、幼稚園ではふつう卒業式や卒園証書はありませんから、デイヴィーには大切な思い出の品となりました。日本語に訳してみましょう。

NURSERY SCHOOL
DIPLOMA

CONGRATULATIONS!

DAVID SMITH

You have completed nursery school
and are awarded this diploma in recognition
of your accomplishments.

Mari Katayama 3/15/20XX　　　Minato Nursery School

---

award 賞、賞金、賞与などを与える　　in recognition 功績、功労を表彰して　　accomplishment 完成、遂行、成果、業績

2. DAVY HAS BEEN SO HAPPY WITH YOU AND HIS FRIENDS HERE.

ジェーンさんが真理先生に、デイヴィーが1年間お世話になったお礼を述べています。

Jane： Mari-sensei, thank you very much. Davy has been so happy with you and his friends here. We really appreciate your kindness and your help. He really enjoyed this nursery school.

Mari： Oh, I haven't done anything. Davy has been so sweet. I was happy to have him. Please tell him to visit us anytime.

Jane： Thank you. Please visit us, too.

Mari： Davy will make Japanese friends easily at elementary school. I'm sure he'll have a lot of fun there, too. Don't forget us. We are always here for him.

Jane： You're very kind. Thank you so much. Good-bye.

ジェーンさんから一年間の感謝を込めたカードThank-you noteが真理先生に届けられました。

March 17, 20XX

Dear Mari-sensei,

　Thank you for all you have done for us. You have given Davy many valuable experiences this year. We will always remember you and Minato Nursery School with fondness and appreciation.

With gratitude,

Jane Smith

Thank you

アルファベットを並び換えて正しいスペルを書き入れ、お祝いの言葉を完成させましょう。

1. Congratulations on your ＿＿＿＿＿＿＿＿ .　　aadginotru 〈卒業〉
2. Congratulations on your new ＿＿＿＿＿＿＿＿ .　　ojb 〈就職〉
3. Congratulations on your ＿＿＿＿＿＿＿＿ .　　natgemegen 〈婚約〉
4. Congratulations on your ＿＿＿＿＿＿＿＿ .　　idwdgne 〈結婚〉

---

have given valuable experiences this year 1年を通して貴重な体験をさせてくれた　　fondness いつくしみ（愛着）の気持ち
appreciation 感謝　　with gratitute 感謝をこめて

3. THANK YOU FOR ALL YOU HAVE DONE FOR US!

このようなときに、感謝の気持ちをどのように表しますか。絵の状況に合わせて次の単語の中から適切なものを選び、空欄を埋めましょう。

candy   help   baseball cards   meal   advice   call   visit   lesson   present   lift

4. NATIONAL HOLIDAYS AND CELEBRATIONS

今年のカレンダーを参考に、それぞれの記念日に合う日付を書き入れましょう。

1. When is Culture Day?   *November 3*
2. When is Mother's Day?   *The second Sunday in May*
3. When is Greenery Day?
4. When is Children's Day?
5. When is Respect-for-the-Aged Day?
6. When is Coming-of-Age Day?
7. When is Halloween?
8. When is Labor Thanksgiving Day?
9. When is the Vernal Equinox Day?
10. When is New Year's Day?
11. When is Marine Day?
12. When is National Foundation Day?
13. When is Sports Day?
14. When is the Autumnal Equinox Day?
15. When is Constitution Memorial Day?
16. When is the Emperor's Birthday?
17. When is New Year's Eve?
18. When is Christmas Day?
19. When is Mountain Day?
20. When is Valentine's Day?
21. When is Father's Day?
22. When is the Doll Festival?
23. When is April Fools' Day?
24. When is the Star Festival?
25. What's today's date?

Practice 年号、日付の読み方を練習しましょう。

July 4, 710= July fourth(four), seven(hundred and)ten

September 23, 1900= September twenty-third(twenty-three), nineteen hundred

December 12, 1957 = December twelfth(twelve), nineteen fifty-seven

April 5, 2005= April fifth(five), two thousand five

---

the vernal equinox 春分   the autumnal equinox 秋分

5. DAVY'S FAMILY TREE

デイヴィーの家系図を見ながら、下記の続柄を示す単語を覚えましょう。

husband ／ wife ／ father ／ mother ／ son ／ daughter ／ brother ／ sister

grandfather ／ grandmother ／ grandson ／ granddaughter ／ uncle ／ aunt ／ nephew ／ niece

father-in-law ／ mother-in-law ／ brother-in-law ／ sister-in- law ／ son-in-law ／ daughter-in-law

David   Linda

Richard   Michael   Jane   Alice

Davy   Carrie

Practice 続柄を表す表現を下記の会話のように練習しましょう。

A：I am Davy.　　(Find Davy and point to him.)

B：Who is this?　　(Point to Linda.)

A：That's my grandmother.

B：Who is this?　　(Point to Michael.)

A：That's my father.　　(Continue making similar questions.)

6. CROSSWORD PUZZLE

これまで学習した保育に関係する英単語を書き入れて、クロスワードパズルを完成させましょう。

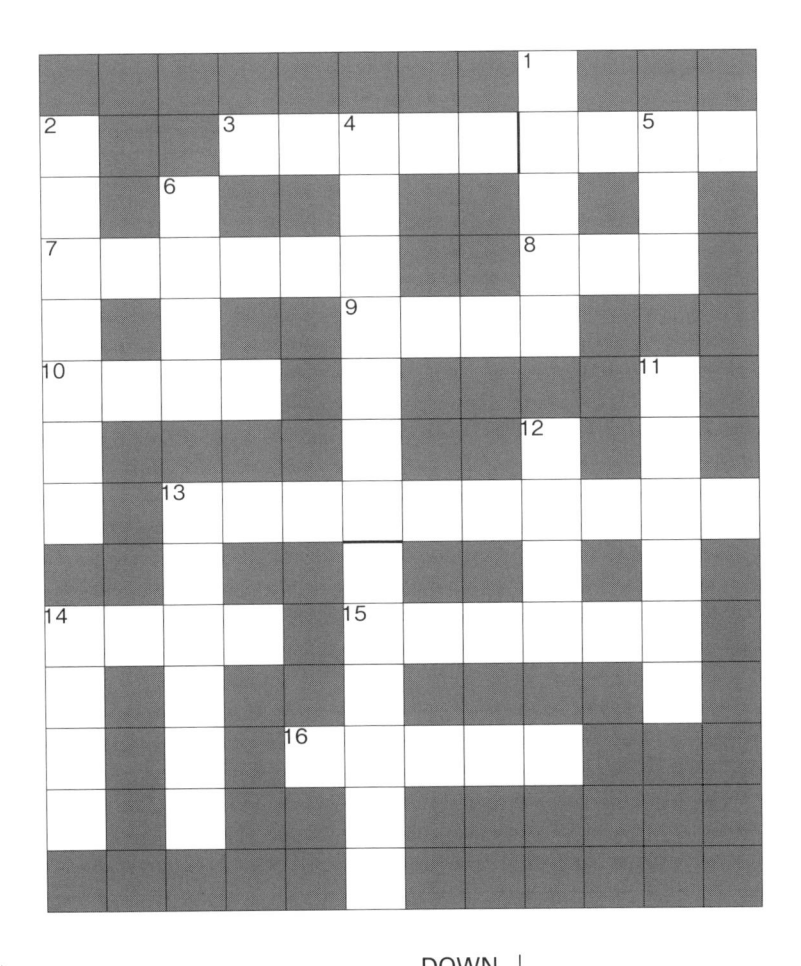

ACROSS →

3. Davy brought extra tissues today, because he has a _____ _____.
7. Be sure to wash your hands after changing a baby's _____.
8. Babies usually _____ , if they are hungry or tired.
9. If your child is _____ , he should not go to nursery school.
10. Which do you _____ better, a sandwich or an onigiri?
13. Every nursery school should have a _____ that is safe and fun.
14. After you feed a baby a bottle, please _____ him.
15. Davy's baby sister sleeps in a _____.
16. The toddlers are beginning to learn to go _____ by themselves.

DOWN ↓

1. After nap time, the children have a _____ and a drink.
2. Davy didn't go to Minato Nursery School when he was a _____.
4. Davy enjoyed his first day at _____ _____.
5. I can't hear the teacher. What did she _____?
6. Babies usually learn to _____ before they learn to talk.
11. In circle time the children enjoy stories, songs and _____ plays.
12. He has a cough. It's probably a _____.
13. Please write about any worries in the _____ – teacher communication notebook.
14. The new _____ in Davy's family is named Caroline.

外国人の子どもの母語について

　母語というのは、子どもが初めて習得した言葉のことを言います。通常は両親〔あるいは両親のいずれか〕が話している言葉が子どもの母語になります。幼い外国人の子どもたちは、母語を習得しようとしている真っ最中なのですが、日本で園生活を行うことにより、日本語という母語とは異なる言語での生活をも行わなければならない状況におかれます。わからない言葉の中で生活をするというのは、不安やストレスがさぞ大きいことでしょう。保育者たちは、そのような子どもたちに身振り手振りを交えて思いを伝えようとしたり、その子どもが興味を持った遊びを共に楽しんだりすることによって、子どもとの信頼関係を築きながら少しずつ日本語が理解できるように援助を行います。そして、外国人の子どもが保育者に心を開き始めると、不思議なことに外国人の子どもの日本語習得が急速に進んでくるのです。そして、半年もたたないうちに多くの外国人の子どもたちは、日本語による日常会話が可能になってきます。こうしたことは、保育者だけでなく子どもにも保護者にも非常にうれしいことです。しかし、日本語の習得だけに目を向けている隙に、子どもの母語が失われつつあるという危険性も生まれてきているということにも気づいていく必要があります。

　外国人の子どもにとっての言葉の習得や発達は、当然のことながら日本語だけではなく、彼らの母語をも含みます。母語をしっかりと習得することは非常に大切なことです。なぜなら、母語は家族間のコミュニケーションを築いていくために欠くことのできないものだからです。さらに言えば、母語は、自分がどのようなルーツを持った人間なのかを意識していく上でもなくてはならないものでもあるからです。もしも、母語の習得が遮断されたり中途半端になってしまった場合には、家族関係に支障をきたすだけではなく、子どもが自分とは何かということを見つめていく過程で、様々な問題を抱える可能性が高いのです。

　また、日常会話であれば、母語も日本語もという2つの言葉が身についているにもかかわらず、考える、創造する、予想するなどの学習を行うために必要な言葉というものが、両方ともに中途半端になってしまうという場合も少なくありません。母語の十分な習得は新しい言葉を学ぶときにも土台となります。しかし、土台のない状態で学んだ言葉は、ある限界以上に深めるということが困難になってしまうからです。

　保育者は、家庭では母語で語り合うことを大切にしながら、母語が習得できるような環境を作ってもらうように保護者に伝えると共に、子どもにも日本語だけでなく、母語をも習得していくことを応援しているのだということを伝えていくことが不可欠でしょう。こうしたことは、本当に些細な援助でしかないかもしれませんが、とても大切な援助なのだと思われます。

障害児保育に関する英語表現

　近年では、ノーマライゼーション＊の考え方が一般的に広がり、保育園や幼稚園に障害を持つ子どもが入園することは、珍しいことではなくなりました。しかし、障害がある場合には、保育者が特別に配慮しなければならないことも多いのです。まして、障害を持つ外国人の子どもが入園する場合には、文化の違いや言葉の問題など、さらに様々な困難があることが予想されます。ここでは、そのようなときに、外国人の保護者に尋ねておくべき事柄についての英語表現の質問をご紹介しておきます。

お子さんは発作がありますか？　　Does your child have fits of any kind?

お子さんは毎日薬を飲みますか？　　Does your child regularly take any medicine?

お子さんは病院へ通っていますか？　　Does your child regularly see a doctor?

お子さんに禁止されていることはありますか？

　　Does your child have any dietary restrictions or physical limitations?

お子さんに呼吸の問題はありますか？

　　Does your child have any difficulty breathing?

お子さんは一人で食べることができますか？　　Can your child eat by himself?

お子さんは一人でトイレに行くことができますか？

　　Can your child go to the bathroom by himself?

お子さんは特別な援助が必要ですか？

　　Does your child need any special assistance of any kind?

それはどのようなことですか？　　If so, how can we assist him?

お子さんはめがねをかけていますか？　　Does your child wear glasses?

お子さんはコンタクトレンズを使ってますか？　　Does your child use contact lenses?

お子さんは補聴器を使っていますか？　　Does your child wear a hearing aid?

お子さんは義足をつけていますか？　　Does your child have an artificial leg?

お子さんは車椅子が必要ですか？　　Does your child need a wheelchair?

お子さんの喜ぶことにはどのようなことがありますか？

　　What are your child's favorite activities?

お子さんが嫌がることにはどのようなことがありますか？

　　What are your child's least favorite activities?

＊障害をもつ人達が普通の生活を営むことを当然とする福祉の基本的な考え方や施策。

Baby Shower──赤ちゃんを心待ちにする
新米ママの出産祝い

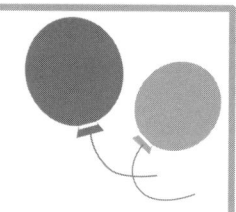

　日本の出産祝いはお産の後に行われますが、アメリカのベビーシャワー（プレゼントのシャワーの意）は出産の数ヶ月前から臨月の1ヶ月くらい前のおなかの大きな未来のお母さんを囲んで行われます。一般的には、第一子を迎える初産の女性のために、友人、親戚、職場の同僚たちがパーティーを企画し、女性だけで行います。

　パーティーの行われる部屋は、赤ちゃんに関係するものが飾られます。たとえば、哺乳瓶を軸にして（ろうそくのように見える）おしめ布を何枚も重ねてできたおしめ布ケーキ。そのケーキには歯固め、赤ちゃん用のくし、ミトンなど赤ちゃん用品が飾られます。参加者に配られるのはおしゃぶりの形の名札、showerということばに因んで傘が飾られたり、ピンクとブルーのテープや飾りリボン、風船の飾りつけもよく見られます。

　ベビーシャワーは妊婦が主人公ですから、お酒が出されることもなく、昼間にティーパーティー形式で行われます。ソフトドリンクのパンチ（オレンジジュース、クランベリージュース、ジンジャーエールを混ぜたもの等）、クッキー、果物、そして、必ずお祝いのケーキがあります。そのケーキのかたちも赤ちゃんに因んで、ベビーベッド、ベビーシューズ、乳母車の形に作られたものなど、とてもかわいらしいものが並びます。

　親しい仲間たちは、思い思いに赤ちゃん用品、育児用品を用意し、パーティーにやってきます。また、妊婦さんが希望する用品リストが前もって知らされ、友人グループで分担して揃えたり、高価なものの場合、共同購入することもあります。この方法はアメリカ人の合理的な一面を示していると言えるでしょう。生まれてくる赤ちゃんが女の子とわかっていたらピンク、男ならブルー、わからないときは白か黄色の淡い色のものを贈る習慣もあります。

　ベビーシャワーにはベビーシャワーゲームがつきものです。参加者全員で楽しみます。たとえば、トイレットペーパーを、妊婦のおなか周りを想像して、その長さに各自が切ります。最後に妊婦さんのおなかにまわしてみてぴったり、また一番近い長さの人が勝ちです。目隠しをしてお人形におしめをする、おしめリレー競争、参加者自身がそれぞれの赤ちゃん時代の写真を持ち寄り、本人とマッチさせて当てあう写真ゲームなど、様々なゲームをします。場の雰囲気がとてもなごみ、パーティーで初めて会う妊婦の友人同士も打ち解けあっていきます。

　さらに先輩ママがお産や育児について話せば、未来のお母さんも安心し、母親になる希望と自信が湧いてきます。また、いただいたお祝いの品に対して、日本のように「お返し」の習慣はありません。ただし、お祝いをいただいたお母さんは、あとでお礼の言葉を添えたカードを送り、赤ちゃんが誕生したら、誕生通知カードを送り、その喜びを知らせます。

 参 考 資 料

Easter——子どもたちはイースターバニーが隠した
卵探しが楽しみ

—毎年、春分後の最初の満月の次の日曜日—

　イースターはキリストの復活を祝う復活祭であり、宗教的な行事です。新しい生命と豊かな繁殖力を象徴する卵やウサギがそのシンボルです。この日、多くのクリスチャンは教会の礼拝に出かけます。子どもたちにとって、この日の一番の楽しみは礼拝の後、家や公園で行われる卵探しゲーム Easter Egg Hunt です。（実際は親が隠したが）、Easter Bunny が隠したことになっている色つき卵を庭や家を走り回って探します。

　クリスマスに良い子のところにサンタクロースがプレゼントを持参してくれるように、イースターには、イースターのウサギ、イースターバニーが卵を詰めたバスケットを隠すという話があります。親は、卵やウサギのかたちをした、ぬいぐるみ、チョコレート、キャンディー、ジェリービーンズなどを詰めたイースターバスケットを子どもたちのために用意します。

　ペンシルバニア州のドイツ系の家庭では、イースターが近づくと子どもたちは、ウサギの巣を作って、自宅の納屋や家の周りに隠しておきます。もし、いい子だったら、ウサギがイースターエッグをその巣の中に入れておいてくれることになっているのです。

　同日、ニューヨークのセントラルパークでも大規模な Egg Hunt Game が毎年行われます。卵のほかにウサギの好物、人参が隠されていることもあります。ホワイトハウスでは、現職の大統領がホストになり、Easter Egg Roll 卵ころがしゲームが行われるのが恒例になっています。イースターはクリスマスとならぶ重要なキリスト教の祭事です。

CRAFTS : HOW TO COLOR EASTER EGGS

1. Put the eggs in a pot of cold water.
   Heat the water to boiling. Boil 15 minutes.
2. Let the eggs cool.
3. Fill several cups halfway with hot water.
4. Add one tablespoon of vinegar to each cup.
5. Add food color to each cup.
6. Place a boiled egg into the colored water.
   Let remain in the water.
7. Take the egg out and dry it off.
8. You can draw pictures on the eggs
   with colored markers if you want.

Halloween——子どもたちは、仮装してお菓子をもらいに 行くのが楽しみ

—万聖節 All Saints' Day の宵祭り All Hallows Eve—

　10月31日はハロウィーン。その日の夕方、暗くなったころ子どもたちは仮装して、一軒一軒お菓子をもらいに近所の家を回ります。"Trick or treat."「お菓子をくれなきゃ、いたずらするぞ。」と言いながらかぼちゃ提灯を持って歩いている子どもたち、魔女や骸骨、幽霊に仮装している子どもたちもいます。みるみるうちに、trick or treat bagは、お菓子や木の実、果物でいっぱいになっていきます。単にお菓子をおねだりするばかりでなく、ユニセフの呼びかけで恵まれない子どもたちのために募金活動をしている子どもたち、独り暮らしの老人の家に慰問に出かける子どもたちもいます。

　ハロウィーンの起源は、紀元前5世紀ごろのアイルランド古代ケルト民族に遡る(さかのぼ)と言われています。ドルイド教を信じたケルト民族は1年の終わりを10月31日と定め、その夜を死者の祭りとしました。それは、死者の霊が親族を訪れる夜であり、悪霊が動き回り人に乗り移ったり、子どもをさらったり、作物や家畜を傷め、悪さをする夜でもありました。そのため、お化けや悪魔など恐ろしいものに仮装し、悪霊に乗り移られないようにカムフラージュしたのが、仮装の始まりと考えられています。また、10月31日は1年のうちで最大の魔女集会サバトがあると信じられたことから、ホウキにまたがって空を飛ぶ、黒猫を連れた魔女のイメージがハロウィーンにはつきものとなりました。

　"Trick or treat."と子どもたちが大声で叫びながら歩き回る習慣は、9世紀ヨーロッパにあったsoulingという習慣に発すると言われています。11月2日のAll Soul's Day（万霊節）には、キリスト教徒が村々を回り、soul cakeと呼ばれる四角いジャム付きのビスケットをもらい、そのお返しにその家の死者のためにお祈りを捧げるという習慣がありました。

　ハロウィーンにつきもののかぼちゃ提灯はJack-o'-lanternと呼ばれます。もともと、魔除けのお化け提灯として、アイルランドでは大カブをくりぬいて作っていたものが、アメリカに来たアイルランド移民が、新大陸では大カブを見つけられず、かぼちゃを使用するようになったと言われています。

CRAFTS：HOW TO MAKE A JACK-O'-LANTERN

1. Wash the pumpkin.
2. Cut a large hole around the top.
3. Take out the seeds.
4. Draw eyes, a nose, and a mouth.
　5. Cut out the eyes, nose, and mouth.
　6. Put a candle in the pumpkin.
　　　7. Finished!

Christmas——ツリーの飾りつけ、
たくさんのプレゼントにご馳走！！

　12月24日、クリスマスイブのこの日、子どもたちは暖炉に靴下をぶら下げてサンタクロースがやってくるのを待っています。夜中にやってくるサンタさんにココアを作って、クッキーを添えてから眠りにつく子どもたちもいます。クリスマスツリーの下には、すでにGrandpa, Grandmaなど親戚や友人が送ってくれたプレゼントがいっぱいです。家中にきらびやかな飾りが工夫され、ワイン、七面鳥、ハム、温野菜、クリスマスプディングなど豪華なデザートがクリスマスの食卓に並びます。

　クリスマスはキリストの誕生を祝うキリスト教の宗教的な行事です。アメリカでは多くの人がクリスマスカードを交換し、この特別な季節を過ごします。しかし、注意しなければならないのは、ユダヤ教、イスラム教、仏教など他の宗教を信仰している人に、"Merry Christmas"と伝えても、それは必ずしも彼らの喜びにはならないことへの配慮です。Christmasということばが入れば、それはキリスト教的なメッセージで宗教的なものになります。相手の宗教が不確かなときは、Happy Holidays, Season's Greetingsなど宗教色のないメッセージを選びましょう。

CRAFTS：HOW TO MAKE POPCORN AND CRANBERRY STRINGS

What you need：popcorn（uncoated and popped）

dried or fresh cranberries, whole

1 needle

70-cm long white cotton thread

1. Tie a knot at the end of the thread and string on the cranberries and popcorn alternately.

2. When your popcorn and cranberry string reaches about 60 cm, tie a knot at the other end.

3. Arrange the string around the branches of your Christmas tree.

このテキストに出てくる主な不規則動詞の語形変化

原形	現在形 - S	過去形	過去分詞	現在分詞
bite	bites	bit	bitten, bit	biting
bleed	bleeds	bled	bled	bleeding
blow	blows	blew	blown	blowing
break	breaks	broke	broken	breaking
bring	brings	brought	brought	bringing
build	builds	built	built	building
catch	catches	caught	caught	catching
cut	cuts	cut	cut	cutting
dig	digs	dug	dug	digging
do	does	did	done	doing
draw	draws	drew	drawn	drawing
drink	drinks	drank	drunk	drinking
eat	eats	ate	eaten	eating
fall	falls	fell	fallen	falling
feed	feeds	fed	fed	feeding
fight	fights	fought	fought	fighting
fly	flies	flew	flown	flying
forget	forgets	forgot	forgotten, forgot	forgetting
get	gets	got	gotten, got	getting
give	gives	gave	given	giving
go	goes	went	gone	going
hang	hangs	hung, hanged	hung, hanged	hanging
have	has	had	had	having
hear	hears	heard	heard	hearing
hide	hides	hid	hidden, hid	hiding
hit	hits	hit	hit	hitting
hurt	hurts	hurt	hurt	hurting
leave	leaves	left	left	leaving
lend	lends	lent	lent	lending
let	lets	let	let	letting
lie	lies	lay	lain	lying
lose	loses	lost	lost	losing
make	makes	made	made	making
put	puts	put	put	putting
read	reads	read	read	reading
ride	rides	rode	ridden	riding
run	runs	ran	run	running
say	says	said	said	saying
see	sees	saw	seen	seeing
sing	sings	sang	sung	singing
sit	sits	sat	sat	sitting
sleep	sleeps	slept	slept	sleeping
slide	slides	slid	slid, slidden	sliding
sting	stings	stung	stung	stinging
swell	swells	swelled	swelled, swollen	swelling
swim	swims	swam	swum	swimming
swing	swings	swung	swung	swinging
take	takes	took	taken	taking
teach	teaches	taught	taught	teaching
tell	tells	told	told	telling
think	thinks	thought	thought	thinking
throw	throws	threw	thrown	throwing
wake	wakes	woke	waked, woke, woken	waking
wear	wears	wore	worn	wearing
write	writes	wrote	written	writing

＜著 者＞

赤 松 直 子 （あかまつ・なおこ）
　　　　和洋女子大学講師 （専門領域 教育学英語教授法）

久 富 陽 子 （ひさとみ・ようこ）
　　　　大妻女子大学教授 （専門領域 保育学）

〈本文・装丁イラスト〉 西田ヒロコ
〈装　　　丁〉 レフ・デザイン工房
〈英文執筆協力〉 Ree Coulbourne（リー・コーバン）

保育の英会話
CHILDCARE ENGLISH 〈第3版〉

2002年10月8日　初版発行
2004年10月5日　第2版発行
2024年4月1日　第2版21刷
2024年12月20日　第3版発行

著　者　　赤 松 直 子
　　　　　久 富 陽 子

発行者　　服 部 直 人

発行所　　㈱萌文書林
〒113-0021　東京都文京区本駒込6-15-11
TEL（03）3943-0576　FAX（03）3943-0567

印刷／製本　シナノ印刷株式会社

＜検印省略＞

ISBN 978-4-89347-408-7 C 3037

This textbook belongs to : _____